PLAIN TALK ON Mark

MANFORD GEORGE GUTZKE
PH.D.

ZONDERVAN PUBLISHING HOUSE
OF THE ZONDERVAN CORPORATION
GRAND RAPIDS, MICHIGAN 49506

PLAIN TALK ON MARK

Grand Rapids, Michigan

ISBN 0-310-25591-0

Library of Congress Catalog Card Number 75-6181

Printed in the United States of America

83 84 85 86 87 88 — 10 9

CONTENTS

Chapter 1

THE PREACHING OF JOHN THE BAPTIST

(Mark 1:1-8)

The Gospel of Mark seems to be written as a significant and authentic record of certain events that occurred in the work and life of Jesus of Nazareth. In other words, the Gospel of Mark is not a story of the life of Christ or a discussion of Jesus of Nazareth as a person. It is not a history of that time. The Gospel of Mark is somewhat like a painting: certain things have been put together in such a way as to give a record of what happened in the life and work of Jesus of Nazareth. This record is important for an understanding of what He came to do.

The report – that is, the Gospel of Mark – is marked by absence of argument. Mark simply tells what happened. He does not undertake to explain and he certainly is not interested in making anything clear to the person who is not a believer. Mark's simple purpose is to state exactly what happened in and to and through Jesus of Nazareth, as though he felt that the plain facts would speak for themselves in any honest, candid appraisal by a sincere person.

At the outset in the first verse of the first chapter we have a strong word: "The beginning of the gospel of Jesus Christ, the Son of God." In these words Mark shows where he stands. He will not be telling only about Jesus of Nazareth: he will be telling about Jesus Christ, the One who has been identified in Scripture as the Chosen Servant of God, the Son of God. At the very outset Mark indicates his own opinion, and will restate it again, that Jesus of Nazareth, whom he knew, is the Christ, the Son of God. He writes that he will talk of the gospel of Jesus Christ. By the word "Gospel" we mean "the message." What then is the message given to the whole world in the name of Jesus Christ the Son of God? We could ask, "What did He come for?" or "What did He come to do?" Any way we ask it we mean: what do we have, what do we find, what will we see in Jesus Christ, the Son of God? This is what Mark will be writing about.

> As it is written in the prophets, Behold, I send my messenger before thy face, which shall prepare thy way before thee. The voice of one crying in the wilderness, Prepare ye the way of the Lord, make his paths straight. John did baptize in the wilderness, and preach the baptism of repentance for the remission of sins (Mark 1:2-4).

There is nothing in Mark's Gospel about the birth and early life of Jesus of Nazareth. Mark starts right in at the point where John the Baptist began to preach about Him. There are no vital statistics given; Mark does not mention the father and mother of that family nor does he describe the appearance of Jesus of Nazareth – how big He was, how intelligent or how strong He was. He starts by telling what happened and he finds the meaning of what happens in the Old Testament Scriptures. To understand Jesus of Nazareth it is important to know the Old Testament Scriptures.

Isaiah had prophesied the coming of the Chosen One of God, the Messiah, as King of Kings. He had predicted that when this King came there would be a forerunner – a herald – the voice of one crying in the wilderness, "Prepare ye the way of the Lord, make his paths straight." Mark points out that this is what John the Baptist did. John did baptize in the wilderness and preached the baptism of repentance for the remission of sins, preparing the way of the Lord. This baptism was the preaching John did: it was symbolized by the using of water.

In the Scriptures water is indicative of cleansing. Water is used to wash away that which you do not want; ordinarily we would say the grime or the superfluous parts are washed off with water. When John the Baptist was preaching, the water he used was an outward sign, an indication, a symbol of what he was doing. What was he doing? He was preaching the gospel of repentance. The people must sincerely repent when they come before God to worship Him. He preached this in such a way that the people listened and were affected by it, and they did this thing. Insomuch as they received his preaching, they were being baptized by him. The use of water in the sacrament of baptism is a symbolic procedure to indicate the true spiritual reality, the message that is given to the heart.

Baptism is to faith in Christ what a wedding ring is to a marriage. A person could be married without a wedding ring and it is possible for a person to wear a wedding ring and not be married. So it is with reference to baptism: there are believers in the Lord Jesus Christ who have not been ceremonially baptized by water. And there have been people who have been baptized who did not really believe in the Lord Jesus Christ.

Baptism does not make one a believer. But for a believer, baptism is a testimony to the world that he is one.

As we think about John's preaching we note he did baptize in the wilderness, and preach the baptism of repentance for the remission of sins. He did not preach "change your ways." He did not preach "get right with God." All this would ultimately be involved. But what he did preach was that the worshiper must admit he is a sinner and must repudiate his sin when he comes into the presence of God. This is preparing the way for any person to become a believer in the Lord Jesus Christ. In the Jewish worship at the time of John the Baptist it was still the right thing to do to bring a sacrifice such as a lamb. But the heart's attitude was what really mattered. In their worship the Jewish people had an understanding that God was God, and He was holy. They held that the Law of God was eternal and if a person broke the Law he sinned, and sinners would die. They knew they were all sinners because the Ten Words given on the Mount to Moses served as a mirror. Now comes the wonderful truth: though they are sinners they can come before God and confess they are sinners, and receive from Him the grace of God sufficient to save them. In the Jewish worship at the time of John the Baptist they were still bringing their sacrifices to the temple. They brought their lambs to the priests and confessed their sins on the lamb. The priests killed the lambs and sprinkled the blood in the temple, then pronounced that the sins were forgiven. But people were doing this in a formal way: it was the thing to do and so they would do it, even though they did not understand or believe.

All the way through the Old Testament the prophets Isaiah, Jeremiah, and Ezekiel preached one thing to the people of Israel, and it was this: there need be no change in the ritual but the worshiper must mean it. In their messages occur such phrases as this: "What do you think God wants? Do you think He wants the blood of rams? He wants your heart." They preached this in various ways. John the Baptist was the last of the Old Testament prophets; and he went around the country with one message: the worshiper must deep down in his heart be really sincere when he comes to God. After listening to John the Baptist they still brought their lambs and their turtle doves, they still came to the temple to sacrifice; but those who obeyed John meant it; they were sincere. They admitted they personally needed the help from God.

Let us bring this principle to apply to ourselves: how does a person make a profession or join the church? Is it not by openly admitting he believes the gospel story; by submitting to the ceremony of baptism; and by committing himself to live as led by God? Yet a person can go through all of that, and still not be yielded to God. John the Baptist would say about this procedure that it would not benefit a person, nor matter one bit unless the worshiper is sincere. He needs to mean it. John the Baptist was a powerful preacher: all Jerusalem came to hear him. But he was a humble man and admitted he was not the Messiah; however, he preached that the Messiah would come after him. He did not dwell on the mistakes of the worshipers, nor on their sins, nor even on their responsibilities: he dealt with the Person of Christ and he promised them that this One he was talking about would save them. He indicated to them that Christ was much more powerful and important than he, John the Baptist. He told them: "I baptize you with water, but He will baptize you with the Holy Spirit."

Chapter 2

THE BAPTISM OF JESUS OF NAZARETH

(Mark 1:9-11)

John the Baptist was a powerful young preacher. He came to prepare the way of the Lord by preaching the baptism of repentance for the remission of sins. The New Testament admonition to all men even today is that they should repent and believe the gospel. The natural man is lost: he is condemned because of his sins: "all have sinned and come short of the glory of God." This is true for every person.

The Jewish religious culture recognized the reality of sin, and also the reality of God's sacrifice for the remission of sin: they knew that sins could be forgiven on certain grounds. The ritual prescribed that the sinner was to come to the priest, bring a sacrifice, confess his sins on the sacrifice, and then take that substitutionary sacrifice and give it to the priest who would slay it. The blood would be taken and sprinkled in the place of worship; then the priest would announce to the worshiper that his sins were forgiven. That was the ritual.

The promise of the forgiveness of sin on the basis of shed blood is Old Testament doctrine. In the course of time the Jews had tended to let this offering of the sacrifice be the end-all of everything: as long as a man brought his sacrifice he felt he was now all right. This had become a routine matter. All the prophets had warned the people that the ceremonial sacrifice must be offered, but it must be followed by sincere faith in the mercy of God. If the worshiper was not sincere the ritual was not effective. This accounts for those passages in the Old Testament in which God challenges the people: "Do you think I want the blood of your sacrifices?" God finally made it known through the prophets, "I want your heart. It is in your hearts that you must come to Me."

John the Baptist served God in the prophetic tradition: he was like an Old Testament prophet. When John the Baptist began to preach there was no New Testament. He taught the meaning of the Old Testament, and his message was simple:

you must repent and be sincere if you want to be accepted of God. In the time of John the Baptist the people who listened to him would still go through the ritual: they would bring their lamb and have that lamb slain and the blood offered, but they did this with true, sincere repentance.

You might ask, "What does that mean?" It would mean that when the man came before God, something of the feeling of Job would be in his heart: "I have heard of thee by the hearing of the ear; but now mine eye seeth thee: wherefore I abhor myself, and repent in dust and ashes" (Job 42:5-6). Or as Isaiah said: "Woe is me! for I am undone; because I am a man of unclean lips, and I dwell in the midst of a people of unclean lips: for mine eyes have seen the King, the Lord of hosts" (Isa. 6:5). Or as Paul, who writes: "For I know that in me (that is, in my flesh,) dwelleth no good thing" (Rom. 7:18). That is what repentance means. It is a drastic judgment of self in the presence of God; as when a man comes into His presence and feels stripped, feels himself standing naked before God, and admitting from the bottom of his heart in all candor and honesty and sincerity: "I am a sinner, I am the one who has been wrong." There must be no excuses, nothing offered in that way.

> And it came to pass in those days, that Jesus came from Nazareth of Galilee, and was baptized of John in Jordan. And straightway coming up out of the water, he saw the heavens opened, and the Spirit like a dove descending upon him: and there came a voice from heaven, saying, Thou art my beloved Son, in whom I am well pleased (Mark 1:9-11).

This account simply states that Jesus of Nazareth came to be baptized of John in Jordan. But in noting the events as recorded it seems clear that these two men humanly speaking were second cousins. Mary, the mother of Jesus of Nazareth, and Elisabeth, the mother of John the Baptist, were cousins and close friends. So it is altogether likely that in the rather tight community where they lived, their sons, born six months apart, would get to know each other. This event here recorded took place thirty years later. They had lived for thirty years in this locality; and Matthew tells how, when Jesus of Nazareth came forward to be baptized of John, John shrank away from it. He felt unworthy, saying: "I have need to be baptized of thee, and comest thou to me?" John, who was filled with the Holy Spirit from birth, would have been very sensitive to what was sinful and what was righteous. He probably knew Jesus of Nazareth, his cousin, as Someone unusual and special. But the Son of God came humbly to John to be baptized, perhaps by way of demonstrating to everyone there, that He approved John's message and was willing to submit Himself to it.

When this happened the Spirit of God came down like a dove, descending upon Him. We should note that this does not say the Spirit of God *was* a dove; while we appreciate the symbol of the dove, there is no evidence that an actual bird was there. Then came a voice from heaven saying, "Thou art my beloved Son, in whom I am well pleased." This message was given to Jesus of Nazareth, who had grown up into maturity: He "increased in wisdom and stature, and in favor with God and man" (Luke 2:52). Later, on the Mount of Transfiguration, where Peter, James and John went with Jesus of Nazareth, a voice said: "This is my beloved Son, hear him." That was spoken to the disciples, but here the word is spoken to Jesus of Nazareth Himself. Here is the place where one can plainly see the three separate Persons in the Trinity.

Sometimes people, in their eagerness to explain the things of the Bible to make them understandable to all (a vain effort!), use language that doesn't fit. Some would claim that when we speak of God the Father, the Son and the Holy Spirit, we are actually referring to three different aspects of the work of God. But here such a claim will not do. In the record of this event Jesus of Nazareth was by the river and John was baptizing Him. The Holy Spirit came down from heaven like a dove. Someone else made His presence known, in the voice from heaven. The voice from heaven, the Spirit descending from heaven, and Jesus of Nazareth here on earth are all three in the same incident at one time. What can we learn from this? We should learn humility.

Jesus of Nazareth did not need to come and subject Himself to the baptism of repentance, but He did it for the sake of the people. He humbly submitted Himself to John the Baptist. He went through this for the impression it would make upon other people.

In your own experience you have probably at times felt that some public worship services were definitely inferior. Did you have the feeling you would not want to belong to that particular group? Your judgment may have been sound, that which you have been hearing may have been inferior, but here is your pattern for procedure: you will find here that the Lord humbly submitted Himself to the situation. You and I will do well to respect these other people – as inferior as they may be. We should take the lower place. That would be humbler and that would be like the Lord Jesus Christ.

Chapter 3

THE TEMPTATION OF JESUS

(Mark 1:12-13)

No doubt many people think temptation implies an improper lust or interest in evil things, in the person who is being tempted. To say that a person was tempted is usually an implication you think the other person was interested in something vile or dirty. We read that Jesus of Nazareth was made in all points like as we are, yet without sin. So I want to explore this idea: I wonder how often this has been understood to mean that He experienced our secret desires, only that He was strong enough not to yield to them? This is actually an error; we have not thought deeply enough. You see, He was without sin. He never had those foul thoughts or impure leadings. Do you think every person has the same sort of mind? Do you suppose every human being has the same yearnings, the same appetites and the same interests as everyone else?

I am going to take myself humbly for an example, in trying to understand this. By no means am I free from evil appetites and desires, but there is something I can tell you: I can truthfully say that in my lifetime I have never yearned for a drink of whiskey. If someone would say, "You don't know what you are missing," I would readily agree. I suspect I don't, and I don't want to know. The point I am making is still clear: I have never in my lifetime needed to resist the temptation to drink alcohol. As a matter of fact, when I was a young lad, before I became a believer, my attitude toward other people was quite strong and I was extremely hostile when invited to drink liquor. So you see actually for me the drinking of whiskey was never a temptation. I am by no means perfect, but I am only using this as an example to show that different people have different ideas.

Now let us consider the case of Jesus of Nazareth, who was without sin. How could Satan tempt Him? If I were to think for one moment this means that Jesus of Nazareth had our ordinary inclination toward lust or illicit desires of any kind, or wrongdoing, I would be in error. If I should think He had the idea of stealing, but that He was just strong enough not to steal, I would be mistaken.

When we look at the records we find that Matthew will tell us of the three temptations specifically. First, He was tempted to turn the stones into bread. We turn wheat into bread when we bake it, and He was asked to turn stones into bread, but that was not the thing for Him to do. Why? Because bread is evil? Oh, no! But it was not what the Father wanted Him to do. He was asked again to trust God to protect Him in case of a fall from a high place where He was asked to go. He was to throw Himself down, and demonstrate that God would protect Him. He answered that the Bible said He was not to tempt the Lord His God. Finally, Satan offered to make Him ruler over all things. Now that was the very promise God made: God promises to give Christ the heathen for His inheritance. Satan tempted Him to get this inheritance quickly by obeying him.

In this temptation everything He was asked to consider doing was not in itself wrong. But Jesus of Nazareth won the victory over all these by following the guidance of the Word of God. In other words, not anything, good, bad or indifferent in itself, was going to be acceptable to Him, but that which His Father wanted for Him. If the Father did not want anything for Him, the word was no! no! Not because that thing was good or evil but because it was not in the will of God.

> And immediately the Spirit driveth him into the wilderness. And he was there in the wilderness forty days, tempted of Satan; and was with the wild beasts; and the angels ministered unto him (Mark 1:12-13).

Although all of the other Gospels have a much longer discussion of this event, this is all Mark writes. When he records "the Spirit driveth him into the wilderness" this is actually a matter of choice of words. The word "led" could be used, and it is so written that way in some of the other Scriptures. But the meaning is clear: the Spirit guided Him into the wilderness and He was there forty days tempted of Satan. Satan tempted Christ at a time when He was alone in the wilderness. It is a comforting reassurance to read in this passage the angels ministered unto Him.

Mark does not outline the forms of the temptations, but he plainly denotes that it happened. The other Gospels supply more detail. The presence of others who believe would be strengthening to anyone's faith, but Jesus of Nazareth was alone. It was when He was alone, when the need for fellowship with others would be most apparent, that Jesus of Nazareth was approached by Satan with the temptations. But angels ministered to Him and the same angelic service is available to believers today. If for any reason a believer should at some time be alone, facing a situation no one else in the world knows about, when decisions must be made, angels will come and minister to him. He will find strength beyond that which he feels he has in himself, because what he has will not be his own: it will be faithfully given to him if he resists the enemy when he attacks.

We must keep this in mind: there is an enemy. There is a devil. Satan is real and he seeks to destroy. He is clever, cunning, wily; and he is malicious. He means to do us harm; if we just watch *him* we will become confused, and if we try to resist him by ourselves we will not to be able to do it. But we can look into the face of the Lord, and He will help us.

Think back to the Garden of Eden and notice how it was done at that time: Almighty God had spoken to Adam and Eve, and told them they were free to eat anything in the garden except the fruit of one tree. In eating of that tree they would die. When Satan tempted them he did not say God was wrong: there was no open contradiction; but there was a subtle insinuation. Eating the food would feel good, and it would look good, and it would set them up.

In connection with deciding what should be done, have you ever considered that the good is often the enemy of the better? A truly believing, decent person cannot be tempted to do ugly, immoral things; there are some people so blessed they are free from that sort of thing. If all I have comes from God, then I am responsible to Almighty God for what I do about everything. I will never be safe if I plan to serve Him my way: I will walk right into trouble, even when I am choosing a good thing.

The Lord Jesus would say: "I do nothing of Myself. My Father does the work." This should be our pattern to follow. We have a clever opponent and we will be tempted at the one spot where we are vulnerable. Satan will suggest a course of action appealing to us but it will not be God's idea. And as surely as we follow Satan's idea we will get into trouble. When that happens we can say in the presence of God: "May the Lord help us."

Chapter 4

JESUS BEGINS HIS MINISTRY

(Mark 1:14-15)

The power of the gospel is to be seen as largely operative in the soul that believes in Christ Jesus. It is not a matter of believing in Him as Jesus of Nazareth, a man. This is the common testimony of history and has no spiritual significance; but believing in Him as being the Christ, the Son of God, according to the Old Testament prophecies and predictions, is vital. If I am to belong to the Lord Jesus Christ I need to know this. The Jews had a long history and a rich culture. In their tradition there were certain prophecies which were to guide them; those prophecies pointed toward the coming of the Chosen Servant of God whom they called "the Messiah."

Now John the Baptist came in that tradition and preached the truth of the Old Testament with power. He focused attention upon what was promised about the kingdom of God. (When we say the kingdom of God or the reign of God we refer to a relationship between believing souls and God, in which God rules: such persons as are under His rule are in the kingdom of God.) The supreme revelation of this kingdom of God is seen in the Person of Jesus of Nazareth, whose personality was under the control of His Father in heaven. This Person is the blessing of Abraham and of all men of faith who have put their trust in Almighty God. The kingdom of God was structured in the Scriptures; but it was revealed finally and fully in Jesus of Nazareth. It was about this Person and about what He was demonstrating that the Lord Jesus told Nicodemus: "Ye must be born again." It is impossible for anyone to enter the kingdom of God unless he is born again.

John the Baptist preached "the baptism of repentance for the remission of sins" (Mark 1:4). I have often wondered how John preached. He must have preached for hours at a time. The Sermon on the Mount was a resumé of what the Lord Jesus was teaching and preaching when He used the text that John the Baptist was using. Great multitudes heard John the Baptist and responded; he faithfully told them: "There cometh one mightier than I after me . . . I indeed have baptized you with water: but he shall baptize you with the Holy Ghost" (Mark 1:7-8).

> Now after that John was put in prison, Jesus came into Galilee, preaching the gospel of the kingdom of God, and saying, The time is fulfilled, and the kingdom of God is at hand: repent ye, and believe the gospel (Mark 1:14-15).

Jesus of Nazareth began to preach when John the Baptist had been put into prison; in that sense one could say Jesus of Nazareth filled the engagements of John the Baptist since both used the same text: "The time is fulfilled, and the kingdom of God is at hand: repent ye, and believe the gospel." The promises of God were all tied up with the coming of the Messiah, who in the New Testament is called the Christ, and John the Baptist said in effect: "He is following after me and you are going to see Him and He will bring it to you."

"The kingdom of God is at hand." This is an important word. When we say "at hand" we mean we can put our hand on it. It was within reach and this was being preached to the people. This was a way of saying to them in one form or another: "You can have the blessing of God. In any kind of situation or condition Almighty God is ready and available; turn to Him; He will take your hand in His and He will save you." This is what John the Baptist preached. These words state the basic thrust of his preaching: "The time is fulfilled, and the kingdom of God is at hand: repent ye, and believe the gospel."

Repentance is a matter of drawing attention to yourself, it is pointing inward. It is saying as Isaiah said:

> Woe is me! for I am undone; because I am a man of unclean lips, and I dwell in the midst of a people of unclean lips: for mine eyes have seen the King, the Lord of hosts (Isa. 6:5).

Job said:

> I have heard of thee by the hearing of the ear; but now mine eye seeth thee: wherefore I abhor myself, and repent in dust and ashes (Job 42:5-6).

All this was very personal: it was all about himself in the presence of God. Paul wrote: "For I know that in me (that is, in my flesh,) dwelleth no good thing" (Rom. 7:18).

These men judged themselves as being unworthy and unfit. We read in his Epistle to the Philippians words of Paul like this:

> If any other man thinketh that he hath whereof he might trust in the flesh, I more: circumcised the eighth day, of the stock of Israel, of the tribe of Benjamin, a Hebrew of the

> Hebrews; as touching the law, a Pharisee; concerning zeal, persecuting the church; touching the righteousness which is in the law, blameless. But what things were gain to me, those I counted loss for Christ (Phil. 3:4-7).

To repent is to judge oneself as unfit. I will not darken that concept with more words. If you, deep down in your heart, know you are not fit, you are fortunate. You are not far from the kingdom of God. But if you think, *I've got some good things; there are some things about me I don't have to change,* you are headed for trouble. Judge yourself. Repent. Look into the mirror of His Word and see exactly how you are revealed in the presence of God – that all your own righteousness is as filthy rags. I am so much afraid that many will miss the point. You may think I am talking about unclean, immoral people. No! No!! Of course it is true for them, but there will be thieves, publicans and harlots in the kingdom of God before many righteous people. Why will that be? Because they have no trouble judging themselves as being unfit or unworthy. Those are the only ones who will be there. If you have trouble judging yourself as unfit, stop looking at other people and look into the face of the Lord.

You may compare yourself with a select group who are really no good. This is wrong. Look instead into the face of the Lord Jesus Christ. I brought this to the attention of a person once and he said to me: "But He was Jesus Christ. I cannot expect to be like that." Then I said to him: "He was in the presence of His Father and you are in the presence of the same God. God does not have two standards. He is the One God in Himself. Jesus Christ fully met that standard, and if you are not like He is, then you don't meet it."

However I argue about it, keep one thing in mind: it is absolutely essential that the first step up is to judge yourself as unfit. Repent and believe the gospel. God has provided a Sacrifice for Himself. He has provided the Lamb of God who died for you and your sins will be forgiven; you will be reconciled to God and your soul will be regenerated. God will show you His grace and mercy. This is the message of the gospel. Repent and believe that you might be saved.

Chapter 5

CALLING DISCIPLES

(Mark 1:16-20)

In the days of Jesus of Nazareth it was the custom for teachers to gather their students from the people of any community and lead them as a company from place to place as they taught. There were no university buildings such as we have now. The teacher might stop under the shade of a tree or he might meet in some man's home; but he would from time to time talk to people and share truths with them. He would seek to share his message, whatever it was, with the community. Certain students would be attracted to him and would come to listen to him from time to time. Sometimes they would linger at some favorable spot for awhile, and persons would join them to listen and often to respond to the message.

From among these interested listeners the teacher would select some pupil, or the master would call some servant, to accompany him and to share in the work of teaching and counseling. These men would serve as assistants or deputies. The New Testament refers to them as disciples; those chosen to be deputies would be called apostles. Many listened and were blessed who did not become apostles; but others were called to devote their entire time to representing the teacher – the leader – to the world, and to share and do some of his work because any man who was going to teach for any length of time would have some contribution to make to the life of the community.

This is the way it was in those days and this is a simple outline of the procedure recorded by Mark:

> Now as he walked by the Sea of Galilee, he saw Simon and Andrew his brother casting a net into the sea: for they were fishers. And Jesus said unto them, Come ye after me, and I will make you to become fishers of men. And straightway they forsook their nets, and followed him (Mark 1:16-18).

This occasion may not have been the first time they heard Jesus of Nazareth, who had been teaching and speaking in public to the people for some time. He saw these men and on a certain day He called them, saying:

> Come ye after me, and I will make you to become fishers of men. (You are to become deputies of mine to reach other people.) And straightway they forsook their nets, and followed him. And when he had gone a little farther thence, he saw James the son of Zebedee, and John his brother, who also were in the ship mending their nets. And straightway he called them: and they left their father Zebedee in the ship with the hired servants, and went after him (Mark 1:17-20).

I might describe the whole matter in this way: Jesus of Nazareth noted some who were listening to Him closely, and He could feel their response to Him. He wanted some of these men as His companions, so He gave them a personal call to follow Him. This involved their stepping out of the jobs and the places they occupied in the community. These early disciples were fishermen with the responsibilities of fishermen. They accepted such assignments as they would be given by Him. We describe this period in the Lord's ministry as the "calling of the disciples."

Jesus is still calling people to follow Him. To follow Jesus does not mean one must go to Africa as a foreign missionary, or to a seminary to study to be a pastor. "Being called of the Lord" actually extends to every believer and means that the believer comes to Him from wherever he has been and turns himself over to Him. Everything the believer does from that point on is done in the name of the Lord Jesus. Whatever use he makes of any money he gets will always be checked with Him because he is His; everything he has belongs to Him. Some believers may feel they cannot go to far distant lands because they have obligations. Whatever the case may be, the issue is this: are they willing to turn themselves over where they are? Are they willing to bring themselves into the presence of God, yielding self and business into His hands, and are they willing for God to be the ruler of everything they are doing? This is what is involved. It is not so much their money or their job as it is what they think about the Lord Jesus Christ, when His approval is the one desire of their hearts.

These fishermen were busy men; but I cannot recall a time when God or the Lord Jesus called a man who was standing still, idle or lazy. These men were doing things. It is so easy for me to feel I have my job, my car, my house and my family, which are all mine. But this is no longer the case if I am a believer. When I hear the call of the Lord I am to turn everything over to Him. The job I have, I do for Him; and the people I meet will be served in His name. These fishermen were occupied; His call took them away from their occupation even though they did not necessarily change their location. Deep down in their hearts these men took Him as their Master. I do not believe they were all unacquainted with Jesus of Nazareth when they were called. They could have known about His teaching. They may have known some of the Old Testament promises. Being acquainted with Him they were called to commit themselves to Him in a definite way. This was a call from Him for a closer walk in obedience to God. There is no report as to what He had preached. One could wonder what He preached; I suspect that Jesus of Nazareth kept on preaching the very things John the Baptist had preached.

Matthew gives a report of His teaching in the Sermon on the Mount (Matthew 5, 6, 7). These people had the Old Testament Scriptures. They had the rituals Aaron and the priests had developed for them. They had the Law and the promises. They knew about these things. There was a certain procedure they would follow and this would not be changed. But they would now do these things, as it were, unto the Lord. Men were in bondage, confusion of mind, distress of soul; and they wanted rest, peace and joy. John preached that God is available, and God is ready and willing to help. But there is one thing we must do: we must judge ourselves as unfit, and let go of everything we have, turning ourselves over to God in trust and obedience. This is the real meaning of believing in Christ.

The Word of God leads man into the blessing of God as he walks with Him and depends upon Him. Being a disciple of the Lord Jesus Christ simply means that deep down in my heart I have committed myself to listen and to obey, to trust and to walk with Him. If that should be your case, you are a blessed person.

Chapter 6

TEACHING IN THE SYNAGOGUE

(Mark 1:21-28)

In the days of Jesus of Nazareth the Jewish people met for worship and instruction in houses of worship called synagogues. It was normal for them to have a synagogue in any place where there were twelve families of Jews. They followed customary procedure in their services which gave visitors an opportunity to witness to the grace of God and to share in the interpretation of Scripture. Such a service was much like a prayer meeting would be with us. It had a certain structure: there were things they did regularly, but there would be times in the order of service when the opportunity would be given for volunteer comments. At such times the visitor would be invited to stand up and share in the discussion that had been going on.

> And they went into Capernaum; and straightway on the sabbath day he entered into the synagogue, and taught. And they were astonished at his doctrine: for he taught them as one that had authority, and not as the scribes. And there was in their synagogue a man with an unclean spirit; and he cried out, saying, Let us alone; what have we to do with thee, thou Jesus of Nazareth? art thou come to destroy us? I know thee who thou art, the Holy One of God. And Jesus rebuked him, saying, Hold thy peace, and come out of him. And when the unclean spirit had torn him, and cried with a loud voice, he came out of him. And they were all amazed, insomuch that they questioned among themselves, saying, What thing is this? what new doctrine is this? for with authority commandeth he even the unclean spirits, and they do obey him. And immediately his fame spread abroad throughout all the region round about Galilee (Mark 1:21-28).

Luke tells about His going to the synagogue: "As his custom was, he went into the synagogue on the sabbath day." Jesus of Nazareth knew all their customs, and in Himself was acquainted with everything and anything that could be said or done in any worship service. Furthermore, He knew the right way to approach His Father. He went to the synagogue every sabbath day and took part in the service. There is a lesson in that for us.

So far as we are concerned, we would be following in His footsteps if we made it a point to go to church on Sunday. Mark simply notes they were astonished at His doctrine. He does not tell us where He was speaking. The custom was for a stranger upon invitation to read from one of the scrolls (one of the pieces of papyri or parchment on which would be written a portion of the Old Testament Scriptures) and comment on it. The word "doctrine" covers the general exercise of teaching and preaching. They were astonished at His teaching for He taught them as one who had authority and not as the scribes.

We may wonder how the scribes taught. You will remember the scribes were the scholars, the people who had read widely the opinions of other men. The scribes probably discussed the various opinions of authors and rabbis in a learned fashion. I remember one such person who was a professor of theology. In the course of his talking about theology he referred to heaven. On one occasion he was lecturing to some college students and one of them asked him if he expected to go to heaven. He replied he did not know and when pressed about the matter said he did not even know there was a heaven! And he was a professor of theology! If I may say so without being invidious, I would think that he would qualify as one of the scribes: widely acquainted with the literature on the subject but never knowing the truth.

The scribes quoted this one and that one and when they were through one did not know at all what they meant. The Lord Jesus Christ apparently quoted no one. He simply read the Scriptures and told how it was. He actually opened it up and showed the meaning. He knew the truth because He was the Truth and He was talking about Himself when He declared it. He talked differently; He talked as one who "had authority" and He did.

Mark does not record anything else about His teaching until we read this: "And there was in their synagogue a man with an unclean spirit" (Mark 1:23). I have studied this and wondered why the unclean spirit spoke up; why there was this interruption in the program. This man with the unclean spirit cried out saying, "Let us alone; what have we to do with thee, thou Jesus of Nazareth? art thou come to destroy us? I know thee who thou art, the Holy One of God" (Mark 1:24). The man with the unclean spirit was in the place of worship. This is no reflection on that poor man, just a recognition of something: if you hold a public service you will invite people – anyone, anywhere – to come, as you should. And you can expect there will be those in attendance who are not free, whose spirits are in bondage. Here is another thing to notice: a person may come to church or Sunday school Sunday after Sunday and never be particularly disturbed by anything. Then someone speaks who believes the Bible and teaches it as the Truth, pointing it out just the way it is. Some begin immediately to protest because this Truth is actually "hitting" them. What is it that hits them? They are made to see their own unbelief as they are brought face to face with an exhibition of faith.

In this case here was a Person who Himself was God. He was inwardly totally yielded to His Father in complete obedience, and before Him was a man with an unclean spirit, a spirit not subject or obedient to God. When this man heard and felt it, the amazing thing was that he knew already this message being delivered was his condemnation. He cried out about it and said: "Let us alone; what have we to do with thee, thou Jesus of Nazareth? art thou come to destroy us?" (Mark 1:24).

Evidently this spirit knew that the destruction of evil spirits was in the will of God, and this One was coming in the name of God. He recognized Jesus of Nazareth as the Holy One of God. It is worthy of note that the high priest did not recognize the Lord, neither did most of the regular attendants of the synagogue; but the demon did and that is a striking thing.

> And Jesus rebuked him, saying, Hold thy peace, and come out of him. And when the unclean spirit had torn him, and cried with a loud voice, he came out of him (Mark 1:25-26).

Some years ago I prepared a manuscript on "The Reality of Demons" and submitted a copy to the late Dr. L. Nelson Bell, a former missionary doctor, for his professional opinion. I asked him from the standpoint of the medical profession whether there was anything in it that could be discounted or refuted. He took time to read the manuscript, and returning it to me he said: "No. In fact, you could have said much more." While he was a doctor on the mission field he often had the actual experience of dealing with demons.

> And they were all amazed, insomuch that they questioned among themselves, saying, What thing is this? what new doctrine is this? for with authority commandeth he even the unclean spirits, and they do obey him (Mark 1:27).

I am quite sure this practical display of power had a definite bearing on the public estimate of Jesus of Nazareth. The people were impressed by the fact that He could control this unclean spirit. Verse 28 tells us, "And immediately his fame spread abroad throughout all the region round about Galilee."

Chapter 7

THE HEALING OF PETER'S MOTHER-IN-LAW

(Mark 1:29-31)

> And forthwith, when they were come out of the synagogue, they entered into the house of Simon and Andrew, with James and John. But Simon's wife's mother lay sick of a fever, and anon they tell him of her. And he came and took her by the hand, and lifted her up; and immediately the fever left her, and she ministered unto them (Mark 1:29-31).

This account is widely known and seems a simple story as we think about it. The company of disciples came into the house of Simon and Andrew, who were brothers, with James and John (doubtless friends), all of whom were now among those who were considered as disciples. Apparently Simon's wife's mother was not in the room when Jesus of Nazareth came in; and they told Him that she was ill. When He laid His hand on her the fever left and then she ministered to them.

Trouble is common to everyone. "Man is born unto trouble as the sparks fly upward" (Job 5:7). Because of trouble man is in distress, and perhaps there is no distress quite as great as the suffering and distress we feel because someone we love is suffering. Some of us are in distress just now, and there will be more suffering as long as we live in this world. This makes the gospel so precious because He says: "Come unto me, all ye that labor and are heavy laden, and I will give you rest." That is wonderful. The gospel is for all men and because of this we have the basis for our broad universal invitation. We say to all men everywhere, "Come unto the Lord." All should come. Whosoever will may come. "And whosoever cometh He will in no wise cast out" because Christ Jesus came for all.

In the case of Peter's mother-in-law, her initial condition – the fact that she lay sick of a fever – was natural. Being sick with a fever is not unusual and for this reason, this particular instance could well represent anyone. Jesus of Nazareth was there because of Simon and Andrew and His friends, James and John.

They believed in Him. He came home with them because of this. There is no evidence that Peter specifically asked for this healing, but we are told "and anon they tell him of her." I am impressed by the fact that in this story there is no record of any request. There is no statement about any expectation, yet she was in real need. Jesus of Nazareth knew her condition, and when they had told Him about her in compassion He moved to help. I want to stress this very notable aspect, there is no evidence that Peter made any specific request. We can have in mind that when we bring our loved ones to the Lord, He knows their need. We may not know exactly what that loved one of ours needs, but when we bring him to the Lord He knows.

What a wonderful blessing it is to have a believer in the family! What an even more wonderful blessing it is to have two Christians in one family. Believers actually have more meaning to their families than is commonly recognized. I do not think Peter was aware that the Lord would do anything, yet he seemed not altogether surprised when it happened. "...and anon they tell him of her." That seems very mild; they did not ask for anything. Perhaps there was not even any specific expectation, but I am sure there was general confidence that He could do something if He wanted to do so. It may be true we do not know what to ask for at times: we may know something is wrong; perhaps that boy or girl of ours is troubled; perhaps given over to fits of impatience and irritation, but we do not know what is really the matter. We should not miss telling the Lord about those loved ones.

Note the simple course of this event: the woman was sick (how natural that was) and the Lord came with the believers into the house. They told Him of her sickness, and that, too, was quite natural. He took her by the hand and lifted her up. There was something He did to her before she was healed, before the fever left her: He restored her to her routine. He knew what He was going to do, before it was done. There may be some people in our own homes who are showing an upset condition because something is wrong with them. It may be that by the grace of God and trusting in Him we need somehow to take them by the hand and restore them to their routine, that we may lift them up. "And immediately the fever left her." This is extremely important. Something was done to her before the fever left.

When someone in the family is in trouble of some sort how common it is for us to wait until they make an effort to help themselves before we will help them out. May the Lord give us the grace to let His Spirit be in us, to let the mind of Christ be operative in us. It may be the thing for us to do is to take hold of them before they are cured.

Thus it was in the case of the lame man at the Beautiful Gate, when Peter and John went up to the Temple at the hour of prayer. The lame man was asking for alms. Peter said to him: "Silver and gold have I none; but such as I have give I thee" (Acts 3:6). He took the man by the hand and lifted him up; and immediately his ankle bones were strengthened, and he leaped and praised God. Peter exercised his faith before the healing took place. In the case of Peter's wife's mother, Jesus of Nazareth took hold of the woman and lifted her up, before the fever left her. How often we are inclined to wait until the fever is gone, and then we take part and go along with these people.

The proper order seems to be that first something is done to the afflicted person by those who have the faith in God, by those who have the grace of God in their heart, and then she is healed. Not so much because of what they did but perhaps because her heart was opened.

"And she ministered unto them." What does that mean? She was restored to her practical duties. This entire incident is impressive because it was handled without dramatics. There was nothing unusual, yet it is eloquent of power and of grace. How we could pray to Almighty God that this would take place among our own people just like this. And we know that it could. If our hearts and minds in our family affairs are given over to the Lord, so that we are with Him and He is with us, things can happen.

Chapter 8

HEALING MANY

(Mark 1:32-34)

In this passage we will see that Jesus of Nazareth worked again in public view. To be sure He always works in the individual. When we talk about His working privately we mean working in the individual in the privacy of the home. When we speak about working in public we mean working in some individual in a public place, such as in a church service or in an evangelistic meeting or a prayer meeting, something of that sort.

"When the sun did set" (Mark 1:32) is a simple way of saying "at a convenient time," when the pressures of the day and the heat of the day are lessened. This suggests something quite practical. Going to a church service or to a prayer meeting, being in a Bible class, sharing with others in matters of spiritual experiences, always results in an interruption of routine activity.

In the Sermon on the Mount Jesus of Nazareth said with regard to praying: "Enter into thy closet and shut thy door." He meant stop everything else and devote your attention to this. So "at even, when the sun did set, they brought unto him all that were diseased, and them that were possessed with devils." The significance of this account is not only that there were diseased people, but also there were those who were harassed with demons (because the word "devil" as used in these translations and the word "demon" are the same word in the Greek). What is important in this statement? The indication of the condition of the people? It is probable that something else is more important than that. Let us consider those who were bringing them: that is the really important point. It is to be assumed these were the healthy ones, those who were free. And so there are healthy ones and the ones who are free, taking it upon themselves to bring the needy ones to the Lord. That actually illustrates my responsibility and yours. Am I well? Am I free? Then I should remember some folks are sick, some folks are possessed with demons: such are harassed, and I know it. I should do something about it. I should seek to bring them to the Lord.

This calls for a variety of techniques. There are various ways of doing that. For instance, I could bring that person to the church services where he will hear the gospel preached. Do it in any way you can, but get that person there. If you have prayer meetings in your church, bring that person. But I do not mean to say this refers only to unbelievers or to people who are not members of the church. There may be people in the church who are sick or harassed – they need to go to prayer meeting and I need to bring them. I need to bring the sick, and not just physically sick. I mean people who have jealousy or anger; people who have hurt or are possessed with demons, who are constantly doing something foolish and wrong that they don't want to do, but are being harassed into it. Those are the people who need to come within the range of the gospel. It is a sad thing when we stand back and wait for them to come. If I don't bring them, who will? If His followers had not brought them, the sick would not have been healed, and the demon possessed would not have been set free.

Souls may be in trouble for at least two reasons: where the word "disease" is used, the reference is to personal inner disorder, and when we speak of being possessed with demons we can think of outward influences. There are people who are inwardly disturbed, and people who are outwardly harassed who need to be brought to God. "And all the city was gathered together at the door. And he healed many that were sick of divers diseases, and cast out many devils; and suffered not the devils to speak, because they knew him" (Mark 1:33-34). Could He do this apart from the personal response of the afflicted ones? I am not sure; it is not specifically described. How would I explain it? I would not try – I would proclaim it. I would tell you this is what happened, and I would tell it to you with joy. The afflicted souls were there because someone brought them, and all the city was there because they were interested. This does not necessarily mean those who were there had faith, but they were interested. Results followed by the power of God through Jesus of Nazareth.

When you think back on those days when He was there, would you have brought your loved ones to Him? If so, then I want to add this final word for you: bring your afflicted souls, the people for whom you care, who are sick inwardly with a spiritual or any kind of disease. Such people are inwardly disorganized and often harassed by outward influences. By all means bring them to the Lord, that He may deliver them, and then give Him the praise and the glory.

Chapter 9

PREACHING THROUGHOUT GALILEE

(Mark 1:35-39)

In our last study we took note of a gathering of many persons who brought the sick and those in distress to Jesus of Nazareth to be healed and delivered. In this study we will note how the plan of the Lord reached out to other communities. But first let us note something extremely important: "And in the morning, rising up a great while before day, he went out, and departed into a solitary place, and there prayed" (Mark 1:35).

Since everything recorded of His actions is significant, we would ask when we read this sentence, why did He do this? Why would He arrange for this time of private, personal prayer? It is vital to look at this scene because it would not have been recorded here, if it were not important. Not every time He talked to God has been recorded, and not every time He talked to His Heavenly Father has been reported; but this report was made for our reading, for our learning. This Person, rising up a great while before day, went out and departed into a solitary place and there prayed. When we think of possible reasons we would say immediately it was not because of any guilt: He had no guilt. It would not be because of any personal weakness: He did not show any weakness. It would not be because of any frustration: He was always able to do anything His Father wanted Him to do.

In trying to reconstruct the mind of Jesus at this point we should read the Psalms. Here is the structure of the thinking of the Son of God as He talked to His Father. We find in the Psalms praise to God – sentence after sentence of praise and thanks to Almighty God! The Son of God on earth is asking the Father in heaven to show Him the way to go. Also there are petitions for blessing. He wants the presence and the blessing of God as He moves forward.

What lesson is there for us in this record of the action of Jesus of Nazareth? For me it is this: if He took time for prayer, shouldn't I? No matter how it might humble me; no matter how

I may be moved to personal contrition and to confession to God. Should I not right now see something God wants me to do? Perhaps He wants me to take time to be with Him.

Notice the time He went: a great while before day. Did He do this so that He would not be interrupted? Notice the procedure: He went out and departed into a solitary place to be alone with His Father. There He prayed. We are not told what He prayed for, and we are not told what He prayed about. That apparently is not the point Mark was making. He was pointing out to us that Jesus took time out and went to a place by Himself to be alone with His Father that He might pray – a great example for us to follow!

> And Simon and they that were with him followed after him. And when they had found him, they said unto him, All men seek for thee. And he said unto them, Let us go into the next towns, that I may preach there also: for therefore came I forth (Mark 1:36-38).

No doubt they had to seek Him but they knew about where He was. They told Him in effect, "You have a great opportunity. Many people out there want to hear You, and they want You to come to be with them." But Jesus of Nazareth answered, "Let us go into the next towns, that I may preach there also: for therefore came I forth." Jesus of Nazareth did not lose His long range perspective even while ministering to the local situation. We can learn from this.

In my own ministry I have, from time to time, met sincere persons who would say: "Why do you want to encourage work in the foreign fields when there is work to be done here? Why do you ask people to give money for work to be done in China when they have not finished their task right here in our own country?" When we look into the Scriptures to learn what the Lord would say it is clear that He has plans to reach the uttermost parts of the earth. To get there, missionaries will have to go and the Lord does not wait until the last person here has decided. When the Word has been declared it is time to go. "For therefore came I forth." That is why He came into this world.

I think everyone should keep this in mind: God will not always deal with a person. "My spirit shall not always strive with man..." (Gen. 6:3). There is such a thing as a whole community ignoring God, so that in time God will ignore them. I think it is possible for a congregation, in their order of services in the whole program of church activity, to leave out the things of the Lord. They can keep that up until the day will come when they will not even have a preacher who preaches the Word of God.

One will find that in that church the people will be dying on the vine spiritually. They will lack personal fellowship with the living Lord because no one is preaching and teaching it to them. It is a blessing from God when a minister tells the people they should turn to the Lord Jesus Christ, and it is a blessing in the community if a church evangelizes the whole community, saying, "Come to the Savior, make no delay, here in our midst He is standing today, tenderly saying, Come." People can continue to turn their backs and one day there will not be anyone to talk to them any more. That has happened and it can happen again. His Spirit will not always strive with men.

The record tells that Jesus of Nazareth went forth on His mission. "And he preached in their synagogues throughout all Galilee and cast out devils" (Mark 1:39). He preached: this is God's method: "The foolishness of preaching," setting forth the truth in words, expounding the promises of God in the Old Testament, exhorting the hearts of the people who hear to respond and believe. This is what Jesus of Nazareth did.

The synagogues were the designated places of worship. The Jews met there to worship God. Many of those men did not know God. Many were not yielded to God, but that is where they went to worship and that is where Jesus of Nazareth went to speak. Humanly they had an interest toward God. This is why they had the synagogue. Such an interest opens the mind to receive. When Jesus of Nazareth went to those synagogues it did not necessarily mean He endorsed the synagogue, but He employed them. They were there and He went to them. Throughout all Galilee this was always His goal.

Demons control the mind. Many persons are affected by influences finding their source in the evil in the world. The gospel also enters the mind. The battle between evil and God takes place in the mind. Preaching affects a person through the mind, through the heart. Because these things are so the heart itself can respond to the gospel. If the heart is involved in worldly interests, if there are any bondages there, the individual from within his heart may resist the grace of God, but the Word of God is powerful, sharper than a two-edged sword and it can cut to the very core of a person. Thus the conflict will go on inside. Almighty God knows it; the Lord Jesus Christ knows it; and the Lord Jesus Christ is able to do the will of God in the heart of those who believe and receive. The preaching of the gospel can open the doors of heaven to the sinner.

Chapter 10

HEALING THE LEPER

(Mark 1:40-45)

The Word of God consists of much more than information. It contains a study of the geography of the land, the customs of the people, and their national histories. Such material may be as involved and have as much to do with the Word of God as the physical body has to do with a person. The Word of God is basically an imperative, a commandment. God speaks to tell me something He wants me to do. He may speak to me and say "Come," when He wants me to come. It is very simple. He may say to me, "Abide," when that is what He wants me to do. He may say to me, "Go," when He wants me to go. Never anywhere along the line does He say "Explain," and never anywhere along the line does He say "Memorize," or anything like that. He calls me to Himself to know Him.

When I hear someone preaching I should feel somehow that the hand of God has been reached out to me, and that He wants to shake my hand. I need to feel as if that person standing there in the pulpit is reaching out to me wanting to shake my hand, so that if I sit on my hands I am not responding. We have been noting so far in our studies the importance of preaching; and we have seen it is by the foolishness of preaching that God will save those who believe. I am now going to suggest that you and I can be helped to understand the nature of preaching more fully.

Preaching is not simply telling the story. Of course, that is important and I need to know the story. It is not merely describing the operation, as to how the Lord does things, nor is it even explaining the meaning of what He does. We will be noticing some of those things. There may be times when He will say, "Consider what I say," and we will think about that, but it will not be the inward philosophical meaning of what has just been said. The preaching of the Word of God will be presenting the commandment of God: the imperative – urging a response.

After reading this first chapter of Mark concerning how Jesus of Nazareth preached the gospel throughout all the synagogues of Galilee, we will again see here in the record a real experience of an individual, showing how the Lord actually brings things to pass. He preached to everyone. Large crowds came to hear Him, but those who received the actual benefit of His preaching and who responded to it were individuals.

> And there came a leper to him, beseeching him, and kneeling down to him, and saying unto him, If thou wilt, thou canst make me clean. And Jesus, moved with compassion, put forth his hand, and touched him, and saith unto him, I will; be thou clean. And as soon as he had spoken, immediately the leprosy departed from him, and he was cleansed (Mark 1:40-42).

This amazingly simply yet profound story is a classic. We do not find any other place in the Bible where there is such a clear description of how the soul comes to God. The leper had a dread disease. It was the rule that wherever he went he had to raise his hands and say "Unclean, unclean," to all who came near him. Then he had to run away from them. That was the law of the land to try to cut down the spread of this dread disease. The leper knew that in himself something was dreadfully wrong; it would kill him. Jesus of Nazareth, who knew the leper through and through, was moved with compassion.

Would you say that His attitude toward this leper was any different than His attitude toward the people generally? I do not think it was unusual. There was special action on His part. This was His attitude toward a repentant person. You may think He did not mention the man's sins. That is true, and in His action He referred to his condition. When a man is thinking about his sins he can talk about his condition, that he is a sinner. Because of this he can be considered to be repentant in this: the leper knew he was sick. He made no alibis; he knew he was sick. He came into the presence of the Son of God and said, "I am a sick person." This is exactly what anyone does when he repents: he comes into the presence of God and says, "I am a sinner."

Jesus of Nazareth was moved with compassion. When He was criticized for being with the sinners, he said: "The people who are well need not a physician." There is no compassion for the person who thinks he is all right. God may be sorry for him – I don't know to what extent. I do not know what is in the heart of the Lord as He beholds sinners, but I do know this: when He looked at the city of Jerusalem, He sat on a hillside and wept (Luke 19:41), having been rejected. He was inwardly distressed because they had turned their backs on Him; however, that is not the same as the compassion with which He looked on this leper. This is my impression and I bring it to your mind just to say this: If you can go into the presence of the Lord and humbly confess you are personally at fault and say, "Lord, I am sick; I have a dreadful disease. I need you," the Lord will look upon you with compassion and He will say, "I will. Be thou clean."

Now that word "I will" has power. That is dynamic, creative, and it calls you into a new being. It is the same Word of God with which He called the world into being. "And immediately his leprosy departed from him and he was cleansed." In this connection I am reminded of a famous leper in the Bible – Naaman the Syrian. Elijah directed him to wash in the Jordan and when he finally obeyed and washed in the Jordan as he was told to do, his skin became again like a little child. And what does that mean? It means that leprosy, that terrible form of skin disease which leaves scars and mars the whole person, when it was cleansed by the power of God, left no scars.

Some years ago an individual came to me and asked this question: "When I look forward now to walking with the Lord, what about my past life? I fear it will haunt me. Am I to have the mark of that as long as I live?" I rejoiced to turn that person to this story in the Old Testament and show her that her skin would become again like that of a little child. We read in the rest of this passage that He strictly charged the healed man not to say anything about it. But the cleansed leper did not follow instructions. He went out and told about it, and a great many people came to hear Jesus of Nazareth. There is no indication he was ever called to account for that. All we have in mind is that it was a very natural thing for him to tell what had happened. I do not understand why Jesus of Nazareth told him not to tell it, unless it was that He did not want to precipitate matters about Himself. It is possible the Lord could do something for me personally and privately which He would just want me to keep to myself. There would be things I ought to tell for His glory, but some things I ought to keep because He wants me to do so.

Chapter 11

HEALING THE PALSIED MAN

(Mark 2:1-12)

The public quickly becomes interested when things happen to affect people. If anything at all occurs anywhere when people are involved others crowd around immediately. The healing of the leper and the casting out of demons were very astonishing to the public in the time of Jesus of Nazareth, and it is easy to understand that many were gathered together:

> And again he entered into Capernaum after some days; and it was noised that he was in the house. And straightway many were gathered together, insomuch that there was no room to receive them, no, not so much as about the door: and he preached the word unto them (Mark 2:1-2).

We recognize that this was the response after He had healed the leper, and after He had delivered the man from the demons. The crowd came and listened to Him preach the Word.

> And they come unto him, bringing one sick of the palsy, which was borne of four. And when they could not come nigh unto him for the press, they uncovered the roof where he was: and when they had broken it up, they let down the bed wherein the sick of the palsy lay. When Jesus saw their faith, he said unto the sick of the palsy, Son, thy sins be forgiven thee. But there were certain of the scribes sitting there, and reasoning in their hearts, Why doth this man thus speak blasphemies? who can forgive sins but God only? And immediately when Jesus perceived in his spirit that they so reasoned within themselves, he said unto them, Why reason ye these things in your hearts? Whether is it easier to say to the sick of the palsy, Thy sins be forgiven thee; or to say, Arise, and take up thy bed, and walk? But that ye may know that the Son of man hath power on earth to forgive sins, (he saith to the sick of the palsy,) I say unto thee, Arise, and take up thy bed, and go thy way into thine house. And immediately he arose, took up the bed, and went forth before them all; insomuch that they were all amazed, and glorified God, saying, We never saw it on this fashion (Mark 2:3-12).

What a remarkable story. My understanding is that this palsied man was what we would call paralyzed. So we have the picture well known to all: a big crowd overflowing the house and four friends bringing a paralyzed man. They could not get in so they went up on the roof. It will help us to remember that the roof was not like the roofs on our houses. The roof was a flat top and it was covered with tiles (that is what it meant when it says it was broken up). They lifted the tiles and "broke it up" in that sense.

When these men had uncovered the roof where He was they let down the bed to place the palsied man in front of Jesus of Nazareth. On their part this was persistent and in a certain sense intuitive: they had planned this action. There is an important truth in all this: these four friends wanted to get their friend to Jesus of Nazareth; they not only cared, they did something about it. They schemed to get that man in front of Jesus of Nazareth. So far this seems to be a natural event, but it is unusual: it does say something about those men. Their behavior was remarkable, and yet all of that we can understand.

"When Jesus saw their faith, he said unto the sick of the palsy, Son, thy sins be forgiven thee" (Mark 2:5). Let's go over that again. When Jesus saw *their* faith (the faith of the four friends) He said to the paralyzed man, "Thy sins be forgiven thee." On the basis of this do you think we are to understand that when God sees the faithfulness of some father or mother praying for a child that that boy or that girl would be forgiven? We can take this suggestion to heart. Do you have some member of the family who has gone astray, whose spiritual life is paralyzed? Do you have some member of the family who shows no response to God? Why not join hands together after the fashion of these friends and bring that wayward soul into the presence of God?

There is another idea here: "When Jesus *saw* their faith." Does that seem strange to you? Isn't it true that ordinarily you would hear their faith? They would talk about it. Or could we accept the idea that they believed because of what they were probably asking? No. He saw it. What does that mean? Their faith was operative: it showed up in their conduct: they did something. Their faith showed in their work. Don't you think it would make a difference if parents were faithful to God in their actions? If they attended church regularly, if they read their Scriptures and would pray, if they gave to missions and were kind to the poor? Do you think their children would not be blessed? It is right here before us: when Jesus *saw* their faith He said to this paralyzed person, "Thy sins be forgiven thee."

Let us look again at the days of Abraham. The Scriptures

record how Abraham prayed for Sodom. In spite of that Sodom was destroyed. But afterwards we read that when the cities of the plain were destroyed God remembered Abraham and delivered Lot. Just think of that!! God remembered Abraham and delivered Lot. Will not that record cause us to get on our knees, to make us sober? Those of us who care for others actually are significant in the whole situation. We can make a difference in a bad situation. God can look at us in our faithful intercession and deliver the person for whom we have been praying.

Certain of the scribes were shocked. "Why doth this man thus speak blasphemies? who can forgive sins but God only?" Jesus of Nazareth did not enter into any theological argument. There was no explanation on His part, no prolonged talk. He asked them a simple question: "What do you think is easier, to forgive sins or to say take up thy bed and walk?" The point being, as far as I am concerned: only God can do either one.

> But that ye may know that the Son of man hath power on earth to forgive sins, (he saith to the sick of the palsy,) I say unto thee, Arise, and take up thy bed, and go thy way into thine house. And immediately he arose, took up the bed, and went forth before them all; insomuch that they were all amazed, and glorified God, saying, We never saw it on this fashion (Mark 2:10-12).

But let us not lose that first thought: "When Jesus saw their faith, he said unto the sick of the palsy, Son, thy sins be forgiven thee." There is another New Testament passage beyond this one in Mark.

> If any man see his brother sin a sin which is not unto death, he shall ask, and he shall give him life for them that sin not unto death. There is a sin unto death: I do not say that he shall pray for it (1 John 5:16).

Normally the sins we are concerned with are not the sins unto death. But let us not miss this truth: faithful people can actually bring wayward souls into the presence of God through praying. God will be gracious, kind and forgiving to those wayward souls because of the faithfulness of these believing people, who are exercised on their behalf.

Chapter 12

CALLING OF LEVI

(Mark 2:13-14)

> And he went forth again by the seaside; and all the multitude resorted unto him, and he taught them. And as he passed by, he saw Levi the son of Alpheus sitting at the receipt of custom, and said unto him, Follow me. And he arose and followed him (Mark 2:13-14).

This is the way Mark records the story of what was going on in the life of Jesus of Nazareth. Jesus of Nazareth was on what we would call a preaching, teaching tour, accompanied by large crowds of people who listened attentively to Him. He had no definite headquarters. His supporters were His disciples. We might wonder what He said when He taught them; and the Sermon on the Mount is an example of that. It is an interpretation of the Old Testament law to show what it really meant. What was His aim in preaching? It seems to me that His aim was to show the human soul the way of blessing from God.

There is no evidence to show that Jesus of Nazareth ever promoted any local community project, or that He ever undertook to change the social conditions in any of the cities in which He taught. He did undertake to do something to the people individually, one by one. He spoke to this one end: to show any man how to be blessed. This can be taken as the major thrust of the gospel of Christ: to bring the heart of man and God into reconciliation. If anyone should question whether He had any interest in the community I could almost ask: "How naive can you be? Don't you know that when the people are changed the community is also changed? Don't you know that if people are not changed it would not make any difference how much you changed the community? Man's trouble – what is really bothering him – is due to his alienation from God."

Man is separated from God; and without God man cannot possibly be blessed. Man does not come to God by his own seeking, according to his own ideas. I am sure there are people in the world who try to come to God by their own efforts. The very heavens themselves declare the glory of God, and any person looking around him will know there is a God. It is natural then to try to figure out what God would be like. Man has a conscience and as his conscience speaks to him, he has a feeling that God would be just and holy. But unless God reveals Himself no man will ever know Him. We praise Him that God did reveal Himself in the Person of Jesus Christ.

But why is man alienated from God? Why is it that man needs to be reconciled to God? What is the basis of all this estrangement? You know it already: it is sin that causes alienation from God. It is not so much some one big sin, or even a whole lot of little sins; it is just sin, it is being out of touch with God altogether. Before long in his alienation the person becomes even an enemy of God. The natural man is not subject to the law of God, neither indeed can be. The only adequate way to deal with sin is by the grace of God through the atoning Sacrifice God Himself will provide. When he is reconciled to God by that Offering, the reconciled soul can then walk in the ways of God. To be able to walk in the ways of God believers have been given the Holy Spirit of God, and the Holy Spirit will work in their hearts.

Before Christ Jesus came into the world to suffer and die for us, and be raised from the dead, the Ten Commandments were given to Moses as a guide for the nation of Israel. Israel made the mistake in later history of assuming that these Ten Words were to guide the soul into doing works that would justify the soul before God. This was wrong thinking. The Ten Words were given to people already reconciled to God to lead them into doing such things that would bring blessing from God. But such attempts to obey the law of God set forth in ordinances never would justify them. Paul wrote in the books of Galatians and Romans that by the works of the flesh shall no man be justified. Over and over again he says very plainly, "By the works of the law shall no man be justified."

Israel erred in assuming that the Ten Words were given to guide the soul into works that would justify that soul before God (Rom. 10:3). This was the prevailing error at the time of Jesus of Nazareth. The Sermon on the Mount reveals what Jesus of Nazareth was teaching. Mark reports how Jesus of Nazareth helped the people by teaching them. These were all Jewish people to whom He was speaking, and He was teaching them that if they really wanted the blessing of God they could have it if they would follow those Ten Words. These were people who already belonged to God, and Paul was doing as the prophets had done, showing them "you have to mean it when you walk with the Lord."

No one knows how often Levi had heard Jesus of Nazareth. It is not necessary to assume this was the first time Jesus of Nazareth saw Levi. It is not to be understood as a case of His coming into this community, seeing this banker sitting there and calling him. We know that Jesus of Nazareth preached from time to time; at some time when He spoke in public Levi may well have heard Him previously. It normally takes some time to build up confidence and faith. Quite possibly, one day when Levi, who had been prepared in his heart by hearing Jesus of Nazareth preach at other times, was again listening to Jesus of Nazareth and heard Him say, "Follow me." When he heard this One saying to him with simple majesty, "Follow me," Levi responded in a simple, elegant way; he arose and followed Him. No explanations and no assurances exchanged, no promises given; Levi did not come to Jesus of Nazareth to get something. He arose and followed Him. It was as simple as that.

I can remember my own call when I was called out of the law office, thinking I was going to be a foreign missionary. I had a contract with the lawyer for whom I was working: I was to stay with him for three years. I wondered about breaking it and then it came to my heart: if I died, what would happen to my contract? Of course, it would be cancelled. I was to consider that when I was walking with the Lord it would be as though I had died. This is the way it must be when we answer the call of God.

Chapter 13

ANSWERING CRITICS (I)

(Mark 2:15-22)

> And it came to pass, that, as Jesus sat at meat in his house, many publicans and sinners sat also together with Jesus and his disciples: for there were many, and they followed him (Mark 2:15).

In every community there are various kinds of persons, different classes of people. There are religious persons, churchgoing people, businessmen, sinners. Some people are known as good (at least they try to appear good), and some are known to be outside the church, and some are known as wicked people. Generally speaking we have the idea that church people should include the good, or at least they should produce the good and they should encourage the good. We associate the good with those who are in the church and making a profession of faith in Christ. and we seem in our own thinking to allow people who are not in the church to live on whatever level they choose.

It is amazing how people seem to feel that if a person becomes a believer in the Lord Jesus Christ he will naturally be good, and if a person does not make a profession of faith in Christ people give him the label of not being good, as getting along the best he can. Jesus of Nazareth astonished the people of His day because He associated with the sinners. He did not go around with the good people, those who were religious. He was with the sinners and the publicans, and this brought on criticism, as we can well imagine.

> And when the scribes and Pharisees saw him eat with publicans and sinners, they said unto his disciples, How is it that he eateth and drinketh with publicans and sinners? When Jesus heard it, he saith unto them, They that are whole have no need of the physician, but they that are sick: I came not to call the righteous, but sinners to repentance (Mark 2:16-17).

I remember how, years before I became a believer, when I was reading the New Testament with interest to learn what it was all about, this statement attracted my attention. I was fascinated by it. I could not believe it; but that is what it says: Jesus of Nazareth came into the world not for the righteous but for the sinners. The scribes and Pharisees criticized Jesus of Nazareth, who was teaching the law of God, for fellowshiping with sinners. This was natural enough and it can be understood. And the Master's reply is amazingly clear: like a shaft of light. If anyone should ask me, "Do you think there are people who are whole, people who are really healthy?" I would answer, "No, but some people think they are." We know from the Scriptures there is none righteous, no not one; and we know, also, there is none good but God.

You and I know people in the church who really think they are all right. They have no need for a physician – they really do not feel the need for anyone to help them. But there are others who know perfectly well they are sick; they know things are not right with them. They are the ones who need help. Jesus of Nazareth told His critics in so many words: "I came not to call the righteous, but sinners to repentance." His critics pressed their questioning. He gave them a clear answer but that didn't stop them. A straightforward answer never stops the critics: one can answer any question but there are always others.

> And the disciples of John and of the Pharisees used to fast: and they come and say unto him, Why do the disciples of John and of the Pharisees fast, but thy disciples fast not? And Jesus said unto them, Can the children of the bridechamber fast, while the bridegroom is with them? as long as they have the bridegroom with them, they cannot fast. But the days will come, when the bridegroom shall be taken away from them, and then shall they fast in those days (Mark 2:18-20).

That was His answer.

There are people who feel that if you are a sincere and honest person, looking at things as they really are, you should be gloomy. That's the way they feel, and from their point of view that makes sense. The truth about this seems to be: if I am trying to measure up to what I think would be required and I am looking at myself, I tell you right now I could get discouraged. And if I look only at other people, taking the newspapers as my description of society, and go by what I hear reported over the radio and on television, I could really be discouraged and gloomy. What, then, can a person do? In the Psalms it is written, "They looked unto him, and were lightened" (Ps. 34:5). That is true to this day. Seeking encouragement from man is vain, but looking into the face of the Lord Jesus Christ is proper.

I could get to the place where I feel everything is lost, but I should look into the face of God above the storm. God is undisturbed. It is true, so far as believers are concerned, the day will come when the bridegroom will be taken away, then shall they fast in those days. There will be times when believers have sadness and there will be times when they are discouraged and could be tempted to be downhearted, when they are crushed under the burdens they have. But if they look into His face all will be different. Worshiping God brings quietness and confidence.

> No man also seweth a piece of new cloth on an old garment: else the new piece that filled it up taketh away from the old, and the rent is made worse (Mark 2:21).

In Bible days cloth was not preshrunk: merchants did not "sanforize" their material. When woolen cloth became wet it would shrink. If a person had a hole in his coat and sewed a piece of new cloth in the hole, what would happen when he stood in the rain? That new piece of cloth would shrink and it would tear the hole bigger. This is what the Master was saying. This is Mark's way of saying what John said: "You must be born again." The great thing is that the gospel is not an improvement of me: it is a replacing of me!

> And no man putteth new wine into old bottles: else the new wine doth burst the bottles, and the wine is spilled, and the bottles will be marred: but new wine must be put into new bottles (Mark 2:22).

This is a way of saying something about wine that many of us do not know. The wine made in Bible days was such that when it was put in the wineskins (the bottles were not made of glass, they were made of leather) it would ferment. When it fermented, the gas would cause an expansion. This would make the wineskin bulge and cause it to stretch. Such a wineskin could stretch once with a certain amount of elasticity. But if men took that wineskin and put more new wine in it, the new wine would ferment and the gas that was generated would burst the stretched wineskin. When the Scripture records the bottles will be "marred" the same word is used as in John 3:16, "Whosoever believeth on him shall not *perish*." We could say in John 3:16 "should not be marred"; and so here we could say "the bottles would *perish*." Jesus of Nazareth is saying to the people that He has come to give sinners something new and different. Because He will do this they are welcome to come to Him: He will take out the old and put in the new. He will not try to reform and repair, but He will replace by putting Himself in their hearts.

Chapter 14

ANSWERING CRITICS (II)

(Mark 2:23-28)

Have you ever noticed how often it is true that those who take no part in a program are among the first and the loudest to criticize? They find fault with the preacher, when they have never preached; they find fault with the prayer meeting, even when they do not pray. Do you realize this is common practice of human beings? Believers should school themselves to expect this and avoid falling into such a habit. It is hard to do but we who believe in Him and seek to obey Him, should be ready to remember that the servant is not greater than his Master. People did these things to Jesus, and they will certainly do it to believers today.

> And it came to pass, that he went through the corn fields on the sabbath day; and his disciples began, as they went, to pluck the ears of corn. And the Pharisees said unto him, Behold, why do they on the sabbath day that which is not lawful? And he said unto them, Have ye never read what David did, when he had need, and was an hungered, he, and they that were with him? How he went into the house of God in the days of Abiathar the high priest, and did eat the shewbread, which is not lawful to eat but for the priests, and gave also to them which were with him? And he said unto them, The sabbath was made for man, and not man for the sabbath: therefore the Son of man is Lord also of the sabbath (Mark 2:23-28).

This is a classic example, and is it not a remarkable story? Let us look at it closely to understand it more fully. "Cornfield" refers to wheat fields. This is not the kind of "corn" we have, which is actually Indian maize. What we call "corn" is a North American plant and had not been brought into the Mediterranean world at the time of the gospel. So when they began to pluck the ears of corn (wheat) the Pharisees saw them and asked Jesus of Nazareth: "Why do they that which is not lawful?" If you have ever gone through a wheat field when it was ripe, you will know how simple it is to reach out and take an ear of the ripened wheat and shred it in your hands. Then you can blow the chaff away, and in your hands will be left kernels of wheat that are edible. This is what they were doing; the Pharisees called it "harvesting."

You and I would say that such criticism was a real case of nit-picking; but such "carping" sometimes happens in the church. When people are prone to criticize they do not have to have a big thing to criticize; any little thing will do. According to the letter of the law as written by the scholars, what the disciples did was actually a transgression. When Jesus of Nazareth heard this criticism He did not quibble over their artificial interpretation or their way of going about it; He faced the issue. There was no attempt on His part to deny that the apostles had actually shelled the wheat and eaten it. He met the problem straight on as they saw it, and asked them: "Have you never read what David did?" In doing so He turned to the Scriptures, which they claimed they were honoring: they were supposed to be guided by Old Testament prophets. He reminded them it was recorded in Scripture that on an occasion when David and his men were hungry, they came to the house of God and took the shewbread (the ceremonial bread used in the sacrifices). No one was supposed to eat that bread except the priests. But David gave this bread to his men on the basis of their *need*. When there was hunger the rules and regulations that were more or less superficial and artificial were set aside. Here the Master expounded this principle to clear His disciples. Then He gave expression to this profound statement: "The sabbath was made for man, and not man for the sabbath."

The law of Moses had specified they were to be careful to respect the Sabbath day and to keep it holy. To do this they were not to perform any work on that day. Their scholars had spelled it out in many specific examples, so there was a limit to what people could do on that day. For instance, one could walk a certain distance, a Sabbath day's journey, and no further. It was also proper to do any work of mercy or any work of need, very much the same as it is with us about Sunday.

Some persons might be very sensitive about respecting the Sabbath, but if they were sick, they would go to a hospital to be attended by doctors and nurses: hospitals can function only because the doctors and nurses, the maids and cooks are doing their work. Those who operate a dairy work on the Sabbath. I grew up on a farm. My parents were careful not to do anything on Sunday, which they felt they could possibly refrain from doing; but we did milk the cows and take care of the milk. My step-mother did her major cooking on Saturday, but there was breakfast to prepare and dishes to wash on Sunday. This needed to be done. Jesus of Nazareth knew this was so; but He stated the regulations set up to protect the Sabbath day from being abused were made with the intention of keeping man from breaking the law; but as He said, the Sabbath (even this very law that they were to rest on the Sabbath day) was made for man and not man for the Sabbath. The idea of the Sabbath day was for human benefit, and in case the human person had need this particular regulation was set aside.

This statement is a stumbling block to many to this very day. Some people would prefer to reduce the whole relationship with God to a series of specific rules and regulations. They would like to act in line with the rules and regulations, take care of all those specifics, and claim all the rest of the day for themselves. There is a subtle distinction here. Have you known people who go to an early service on Sunday to have the rest of the day to themselves? Do you realize some people will even go to church to feel righteous? Some may go to make friends, or to gain contacts with people for business purposes. Don't you think God knows about that? This is something like the distinction between being polite and being courteous. Those are two different things: a person may be polite with people he does not even like, but courtesy is a matter of the heart.

The Pharisees had added all sorts of regulations to the Old Testament law. Some were so specific they almost sound funny. Jesus of Nazareth did not disregard these regulations; I do not know of any place where it is recorded He broke any of them, unless it was absolutely necessary to do so in serving His God. But such attention to regulations can be a real snare. We could set up a whole religious system of living in which regulation after regulation is kept, and this could all be a matter of the flesh. A person could do this as a human being. He could go to church and sing his songs, and hate the people who were in the church with him. He could in heart and mind despise the poor, and flatter the rich, right while he was in church. Don't you think God knows those things? He looks down into the heart.

Jesus of Nazareth simply refused to be impressed with their criticism, and distinctly told them they were wrong when they criticized His disciples for shelling out the wheat to eat. The disciples were hungry, and because they were hungry and had need, the rules about harvesting at this point could be set aside.

Chapter 15

HEALING ON THE SABBATH

(Mark 3:1-6)

It is one of the strange sad facts about the history of the gospel that it is often the experience of earnest, sincere believers to arouse opposition and hostility in spite of carefulness in their conduct. Regardless of how meek and humble such believers may be, they may be just unacceptable to some other people. It seems almost incredible that anyone who humbly testifies to the grace of God and to the joy of believing in the Lord Jesus Christ should encounter such opposition. The opposition may start in derision, in mockery, and end in hatred and bitterness. This happens over and over again.

Jesus of Nazareth came unto His own and His own received Him not. He came to give His life a ransom for many who turned their backs on Him. After He had been preaching and serving awhile they became His enemies.

> And he entered again into the synagogue; and there was a man there which had a withered hand. And they watched him, whether he would heal him on the sabbath day; that they might accuse him. And he saith unto the man which had the withered hand, Stand forth. And he saith unto them, Is it lawful to do good on the sabbath days, or to do evil? to save life, or to kill? But they held their peace. And when he had looked round about on them with anger, being grieved for the hardness of their hearts, he saith unto the man, Stretch forth thine hand. And he stretched it out: and his hand was restored whole as the other. And the Pharisees went forth, and straightway took counsel with the Herodians against him, how they might destroy him (Mark 3:1-6).

This is an amazing record. It was the Sabbath day and the custom of the people on the Sabbath day was to go to the place of public worship. Jesus of Nazareth came to the synagogue as was His custom. There was a man there who had a withered hand, and was in need. The opponents of Jesus watched Him to see whether He would heal on the Sabbath day that they might accuse Him. Apparently they were not interested in the man with the withered hand. What they cared about was to find some way they could trap Jesus of Nazareth to put Him in the wrong. Jesus of Nazareth was always humble, and always meek: but you can keep in mind whenever you read in Matthew, Mark, Luke and John about Him, never at any time did He fail to stand up for what He was presenting. So they came to see what He would do. He made it clear. He said to this man who had the withered hand, "Stand forth." He met this thing head-on. Then He asked them, "Is it lawful (according to Scripture) to do good on the sabbath days, or to do evil?" Is it according to the teaching of Moses that you should do good on the Sabbath day or would he have you do evil?

The law of the Old Testament indicated that if it was a work of mercy you could do it on the Sabbath. One illustration in particular was that if a person should walk along a country road and see his neighbor's ox in the ditch on the Sabbath he should pull him out. Pulling a steer or a cow out of a mudhole involves real work. So Jesus stands before them, asking them if they want Him to let the man stay as he is, and thus leave that ox in the ditch to die. They were speechless with anger. I sometimes feel as though in this case one could say He rubbed their error right into their faces.

Sometimes we wonder if there was ever such a thing as anger in Jesus of Nazareth. When we read, "And when he had looked round about on them with anger," we wonder if that anger is to be associated with righteousness. Can anger belong in a spiritual frame of mind? Obviously the word is "yes." There are some things in this world that if they do not arouse anger in me, something is wrong with me! God is angry with the wicked every day. The Lord Jesus was angered with them, being grieved for the hardness of their hearts. They would have allowed the crippled man stay in that condition before they would admit they were wrong, and agree to allow Jesus of Nazareth to heal him.

> And when he had looked round about on them with anger, being grieved for the hardness of their hearts, he saith unto the man, Stretch forth thine hand. And he stretched it out: and his hand was restored whole as the other (Mark 3:5).

But this action led to this reaction:

> And the Pharisees went forth, and straightway took counsel with the Herodians against him, how they might destroy him (Mark 3:6).

Think of that. When there was a need and He came to supply

that need, there were people who actually did not care about that man in need. They wanted only to catch Jesus of Nazareth in some position where they could accuse Him of having broken the law.

There will be people who will watch us critically if we bear our witness and testimony for the Lord Jesus Christ. Maybe I am doing church visitation; maybe I teach a Sunday school class. Maybe I work with young people in large groups. Whatever Christian activity I may be doing, let me remember to be very careful how I conduct myself. There will be people watching me and if they can find fault with me they will do it, even when I have done nothing wrong. Jesus of Nazareth knew they would do this but He did not hesitate to face the issue. He knew they would attempt to trap Him. In effect, He said to this man, "Stand forth." Then He turned to them, "Now, are you going to raise a question about this? Is it lawful to do good on the Sabbath day?" As a matter of fact it was lawful, and they knew it and that made them hold their peace. "And when he had looked round about on them with anger, being grieved for the hardness of their hearts. . . ."

Don't misunderstand me: I have great appreciation for the meekness and mildness of Jesus of Nazareth. He says:

> Come unto me, all ye that labor and are heavy laden, and I will give you rest. Take my yoke upon you, and learn of me; for I am meek and lowly in heart: and ye shall find rest unto your souls (Matt. 11:28-29).

I know He was reviled and He reviled not again. When men said things against Him He never answered them. But here was the case where a poor man was in trouble and there were people opposing His healing this man because they did not like Jesus of Nazareth. He did not hesitate: "Stretch forth thine hand." The man was actually healed. Even so His critics still would not concede that Jesus of Nazareth was right. They still opposed Him.

"And the Pharisees went forth, and straightway took counsel with the Herodians against him." That opposition is active today. We find it whoever we may be and wherever we may go. There is no way to escape it. Criticism will come but the guidance is clear: move straight ahead. You may be meek, you may be humble, but don't be weak. Step right out and go forward – as you do. The opposition that will come to you is the opposition that would come against the Lord Jesus Christ Himself and the only way to face that to the glory of God is head-on. You may suffer for it (they eventually killed the Lord Jesus for it), but you will glorify God.

Chapter 16

PREACHING TO THE MULTITUDES

(Mark 3:7-12)

There is no prospect that the gospel can be preached anywhere without meeting criticism and arousing opposition. People do not want circumstances changed. They can accept the fact that some people believe in Christ and pray to God; that is all right. Certain others do not accept Christ and do not pray; this is also all right. They have that all settled in their minds. But they resent and oppose any change; they do not want any unbelievers to become believers and upset the balance of the community.

But the will of God is that all men should hear and know what is available, so God moves His obedient servants to proclaim the gospel in the face of opposition.

> But Jesus withdrew himself with his disciples to the sea: and a great multitude from Galilee followed him, and from Judea, and from Jerusalem, and from Idumea, and from beyond Jordan; and they about Tyre and Sidon, a great multitude, when they had heard what great things he did, came unto him. And he spake to his disciples, that a small ship should wait on him because of the multitude, lest they should throng him. For he had healed many; insomuch that they pressed upon him for to touch him, as many as had plagues. And unclean spirits, when they saw him, fell down before him, and cried, saying, Thou art the Son of God. And he straitly charged them that they should not make him known (Mark 3:7-12).

This gives us a simple record of how it was going in those days. When the Pharisees joined with the Herodians to plan how to destroy Him, Jesus withdrew with His disciples to the sea. We can call that strategic withdrawal. Many of us could learn from this. Suppose you are in a situation where you have declared the Word of God and opposition is aroused (this would not be surprising). Such opposition may be based on anything: people don't like the way you talk; they don't like the way you dress; they don't like the way you do your hair and they don't like the way you look. They just don't want you around. And when this opposition developed we should note carefully: the Lord withdrew. This is a hard thing for many of us to accept. The idea of turning and walking away from it does not appeal to us all. Many of us are dogmatic: we are ready to stay there. We want to show them they can't run us out. We may be inclined to stay there: to waste our time, our energy, our spirit and our opportunities, bumping our heads against a stone wall when there is no door there. We may need to learn from this: Jesus withdrew Himself with His disciples to the sea.

Early in the Bible we read: "My spirit shall not always strive with man" (Gen. 6:3). This is worth noting. Jesus of Nazareth avoided open confrontation with His enemies. He could have brought everything to a climax right then, but it was too early. He could have precipitated a final crisis; it was too early for that. He had much work left to do. The time would come when He would be crucified, and when that time came He would know it from the Father, and He would walk into it with peace, and accept the way which the will of His Father laid out for Him. But this was not the time. Believers should keep in mind when they are in a difficult situation trying to get something done, that it may not be the place or the time for a showdown.

> . . . and a great multitude from Galilee followed him, and from Judea, and from Jerusalem, and from Idumea, and from beyond Jordan; and they about Tyre and Sidon, a great multitude, when they had heard what great things he did, came unto him (Mark 3:7-8).

We might ask ourselves this question. Do we think that in the proclamation of the gospel there should be publicity? Should people tell about what the Lord has done? And the answer must be a very simple "Yes." Believers should tell about it. There is much spiritual lethargy in many groups of believing, professing people because of lack of personal witnessing. One of the reasons why in many cases there seems so little activity and so little interest in the congregational fellowship is that no one ever says anything about what the Lord has done for him or for her. If church members would make it their purpose to let others know when they had been blessed of God, it would lift the tone of church fellowship to an inspiring level. If individuals would get up and say what the Lord had done during the past week (in answering prayer and in the helping of the believer when he was in trouble), the church would be crowded with persons seeking similar help from God. People will go to see a fire. That is a common human trait. It does not make any difference what is burning; if there is a big fire, there will be a big crowd. So far as having people come to hear the gospel, let the flames of personal testimony reach to high heaven, and sinners will come.

Do you know why this great multitude came? Because they had heard about Jesus of Nazareth and the work He had done. On this occasion they were about to crowd Him into the sea because there were so many of them. And here we see how to honor the Lord: talk, tell what He has done. Even if you must get a little boat to stand in.

> . . . they pressed upon him for to touch him, as many as had plagues. And unclean spirits, when they saw him, fell down before him, and cried, saying, Thou art the Son of God. And he straitly charged them that they should not make him known (Mark 3:10-12).

Souls were blessed and they talked about it. Diseases were healed and they praised God. Bondage was broken, souls were delivered and they testified. He became widely known and as surely as He was widely known, many came and when many came, many were blessed. That is the way it will go. Now we can understand why He would tell His disciples: "Go ye into all the world and tell what things I have commanded you."

Chapter 17

ORDAINING THE APOSTLES

(Mark 3:13-19)

We often hear about persons going into Christian service as though this was an activity that any well-meaning person could undertake as one would undertake a profession. Men seem to feel that a person could make his choice and decide whether he is going to go into law or into medicine or, as some used to say, go into the church (the ministry) as though it were something a man could undertake for personal reasons. It is quite common to hear some interested person saying to some young man, "Have you ever thought of the ministry?" as if this were something he could choose for himself. No doubt some well-meaning young people consider going into the ministry as a way of helping others. They can see themselves doing something for the poor, for the confused, and helping those who are in trouble or perhaps ministering to those who are under addiction of some sort. There is always the danger the individual may choose such a course of action on his own initiative.

I well remember when I was facing the thought of making my decision whether I should leave the law office to go to the foreign field, and I can tell you one thing I dreaded: the thought that I might be considering the mission field as something I might choose to do. It probably would have been easy to make application to some mission board, to be examined and approved, and then find myself out in the heart of Africa only to realize it was my idea. That scared me. I remembered so well the words of the Lord Jesus:

> Ye have not chosen me, but I have chosen you, and ordained you, that ye should go and bring forth fruit, and that your fruit should remain: that whatsoever ye shall ask of the Father in my name, he may give it you (John 15:16).

That was very meaningful to me.

"And he goeth up into a mountain, and calleth unto him whom he would: and they came unto him" (Mark 3:13). Notice the process. It was His idea, and He chose the ones He wanted to have come. This was a new idea. It does not mean He did not know about Simon before He ever saw him or that He had never thought about James or John. God knows all things; He knows the end from the beginning. When I was facing the idea that perhaps the Lord wanted me to go to the foreign field, it was not at that particular time He had first thought of me. For me to understand intelligently was for me to recognize that He had been preparing me for this from the first. He would have known from the beginning.

> And he ordained twelve, that they should be with him, and that he might send them forth to preach, and to have power to heal sicknesses, and to cast out devils: and Simon he surnamed Peter; and James the son of Zebedee, and John the brother of James; and he surnamed them Boanerges, which is, The sons of thunder: and Andrew, and Philip, and Bartholomew, and Matthew, and Thomas, and James the son of Alpheus, and Thaddeus, and Simon the Canaanite, and Judas Iscariot, which also betrayed him: and they went into a house (Mark 3:14-19).

When God was calling him, Jeremiah hesitated, saying he was too young. "Then the word of the Lord came unto me, saying, Before I formed thee in the belly I knew thee; and before thou camest forth out of the womb I sanctified thee, and I ordained thee a prophet unto the nations" (Jer. 1:4-5). Could you believe such would be true not only of a prophet, but also this is the way it is with each of us? The Lord knows us from the beginning and He shapes everything toward the end He has in mind. When we speak about the call of the Lord we need not think only of something that happens suddenly. It might come to a climax suddenly, and it might actually come into my consciousness that way. As I reflect upon the matter I might even be able to see the hand of God; but far beyond my understanding the Scriptures will reveal to me that God knew all the time what He was going to do with me. When we read: "and calleth unto him whom he would," it shows this was His idea. Mark simply reports "they came unto him" as they were. Apparently there was no correction made, no adjustment, no special preparation of any kind; they came immediately just as they were.

I should learn from this that if I ever have the feeling the Lord is calling me, He does not want me to go first and do something and then come. As a matter of fact the Scriptures do teach something like that: if I am holding in my heart something against someone, so that I actually have a feeling of antagonism toward that person, I should first go and be reconciled to my brother and then come and offer my gift. But when the Lord calls nothing is necessary there.

"He ordained twelve." He set them aside for a special purpose. What were they to do? Three things: first, they should be with Him. Mind you, that is not simple. They would have to shed many things. Second: they were to be sent forth to convey a message. This they could do with words, they could do that in the manner of their actions. They were to communicate a message, and that message was not just information. The Word of God is never just so much information about things; there is always involved in it a commandment, asking for a response. That is the significance of preaching, and that is how preaching differs from teaching. ". . . that he might send them forth to preach." They were to address the whole community as if they were reaching out their hand and inviting people to come and take it. Third: they were "to have power to heal sicknesses, and to cast out devils." Do you recognize the difference between those two things? Sickness is from within. When something is wrong inside of me and certain aspects of my inner functioning are not right, I need to be healed. The disciples would have power to heal and to cast out demons.

Demons are influences affecting me from the outside in such a way that I am not my own man. I am being influenced by others from the outside. The preaching these apostles were to do would have the power to heal and to deliver.

> And Simon he surnamed Peter; and James the son of Zebedee, and John the brother of James; and he surnamed them Boanerges, which is, The sons of thunder (Mark 3:16-17).

He actually called them by different names which suggests changes in their personalities. They had their natural capacities, but apparently He added new abilities. He gave them these just as He gave Peter stability, so He gave James and John power to preach. Finally the list ends by saying: "And Judas Iscariot, which also betrayed him."

There is a truth here I should soberly note: being included among His servants does not guarantee a man's heart will be right. It is a great privilege to be one of God's servants, but that is no guarantee that my heart will be right. That must come from the Lord Himself.

Chapter 18

ANSWERING THE CRITICS

(Mark 3:20-30)

Sometimes the presentation of the gospel will be questioned and hindered by the well-meaning but mistaken notions of friends. Sometimes the believer will be bearing witness, perhaps visiting persons to talk to them, perhaps giving personal testimony, and friends will come along and begin to urge the witness: "You are going too far; you should not do that." It can happen under such circumstances that a man's friends who think they are helping him can actually turn out to be his worst enemies because they get in his way. This can be understood because a man's friends are human, and because of the limitations of human understanding. People may be sincere, they may be kind and sympathetic, but they can be terribly wrong.

> And the multitude cometh together again, so that they could not so much as eat bread. And when his friends heard of it, they went out to lay hold on him: for they said, He is beside himself (Mark 3:20-21).

What does it mean to "lay hold on Him"? They tried to restrain Him. They went out to Him and said in effect, "Let's take it easy. Go slow. You are going overboard on this matter." Today men would say, "He is unbalanced; he has gone off the deep end." As the record goes on from there it is not only His friends who feel this way but the scribes, i.e. "scholars." There are specialists who study human nature and who seek to explain what happens in the human being. They probe into the functioning of the mind and heart, and come up with various ideas in the fields of psychology and sociology. Sometimes they put all this together in techniques of psychiatry, as they try to explain away spiritual things. If someone has a profound experience of the Lord they may say: "His conscience is bothering him." When some person has a definite feeling of conviction of sin, they will offer a human, natural explanation. I remember hearing such a specialist say once that sin is just a rationalization of the inferiority complex.

To have the significance of the inner experience blurred in such words is a human reaction. That is all it is beneath the surface. Men come up with ideas no one knows anything about, and make them sound so possible and so impressive that oftentimes a person is actually influenced by these accounts. As a matter of fact as we read this account we notice that no one questioned His works. This is amazing. No one denied what He had done. The reality of the accomplishments of the preaching and teaching, of the exercise of the power of the Lord Jesus Christ was undeniable. It was obvious. People were being healed and delivered. Men without faith in God, who did not believe in the promises of God, could not understand what they saw. They tried to explain it away in some way, and so they offered hypothetical theories to account for what happened. "And the scribes which came down from Jerusalem said, He hath Beelzebub, and by the prince of the devils casteth he out devils" (Mark 3:22).

I suspect many who read that phrase will be as I was. I had never thought of "Beelzebub" and I do not know what they meant by that. The Bible seems to imply that was the name given to the outstanding servant of Satan who was called the prince of devils. Thus they were saying that Jesus of Nazareth was "in cahoots" with the devil. Some critics today who do not believe in the devil have other ways of explaining such experience.

It was obvious that deliverances were occurring; people were actually being set free. How could those smart men propose the true reason when they did not believe in God? They said Jesus of Nazareth was in league with the devil, working some "shenanigans" with unseen psychic powers. It is indeed salutary to notice how He faced this insinuation:

> And he called them unto him, and said unto them in parables, [He used illustrations to get His ideas across, reasoning from a logical point of view] How can Satan cast out Satan? And if a kingdom be divided against itself, that kingdom cannot stand. And if a house be divided against itself, that house cannot stand. And if Satan rise up against himself, and be divided, he cannot stand, but hath an end. No man can enter into a strong man's house, and spoil his goods, except he will first bind the strong man; and then he will spoil his house (Mark 3:23-27, bracketed commentary mine).

Jesus of Nazareth said in effect: "If you see me deliver a man who is under bondage, a man who has been possessed with a demon, you are to understand I have power over him. I go into his house and turn that man loose."

At no point along the line did He explain how He did these things. Arguing with people who make foolish or subtle, sophisticated explanations in which God is left out does not show the truth of the gospel. But it does expose the logical fallacy to the people themselves, and this is desirable. This is what Paul told Timothy to do:

> But foolish and unlearned questions avoid, knowing that they do gender strifes. And the servant of the Lord must not strive; but be gentle unto all men, apt to teach, patient, in meekness instructing those that oppose themselves; if God peradventure will give them repentance to the acknowledging of the truth (2 Tim. 2:23-25).

We never know when someone of those men who is so mistaken might be willing to follow the truth, and if we show them the truth they might turn. We do not want to alienate them and so we talk to them in a way they can follow, a reasoning way. The Lord used logic to show the fallacy of their position so that if there should be any of them willing he could break out of the snare. This is our guidance so far as you and I are concerned. When we are dealing with critics there will be times when the criticism itself in the things they say is actually foolish. We can reason with them, not to show what is true because they are not ready for that, but to show them what is wrong about what they say. This is what Jesus of Nazareth did.

> Verily I say unto you, All sins shall be forgiven unto the sons of men, and blasphemies wherewith soever they shall blaspheme: but he that shall blaspheme against the Holy Ghost hath never forgiveness, but is in danger of eternal damnation: because they said, He hath an unclean spirit (Mark 3:28-30).

What is the significance of this? They had actually slandered what Jesus of Nazareth had done. He had exercised the power of God, and they were saying, "He is in league with the devil." Thus they slandered the work of the Holy Spirit of God and the Master warned them that anyone who does that will never be forgiven. We can see how this is involved. The Holy Spirit deals with me about the things of the Lord. If I have inward prompting to turn to God, and then I let someone tell me those inward promptings are just psychological movements from within my own being (that my own mind and heart is thinking those things), that man is doing me wrong. And what is more that man can incur the wrath of God. It is an exceedingly dangerous thing to slander the work of the Holy Spirit in anyone. We should be extremely careful that we do not slander the work of the Holy Spirit of God in any man's soul, even if that man is not doing things our way.

Chapter 19

WHO IS MY MOTHER?

(Mark 3:31-35)

Studies in human nature have revealed that a person needs attachment to others to develop his own stability and strength of character. This means that if anyone is to become strong and satisfied in life there must be other people around him in whom he has personal confidence and with whom he has fellowship. It is not good for man to be alone: to have relationship with others is a good thing. First of all, a man is related to himself and he has in himself some attitude toward himself. In the second place, he is related to society; the people around him. In the third place, he is related to his God. The three are arranged in this way, moving from the least through the more to the most. There is no doubt that for many people their supreme attachment is in number two. Of course, there are some people who get intrigued with themselves and are, therefore, inclined to focus upon self; but they really are not wise because being centered in self they soon drift around from place to place without any real strength. Some people get just as far as their society goes, as the people who are with them. When we think about society we think about their home, or their outstanding leaders, or the people in whom they are interested, e.g. their sweethearts; and these are the ones in whom they find their interest and their satisfaction. If those things are constant they can have strong characters.

The gospel of Jesus Christ brings to our attention the supremacy of number three in that list: God. God is more important than any other; self (number one) the least important; society (number two), the people round one, is more important. But God is also all round him. This is brought out in these words uttered by Jesus of Nazareth:

> He that loveth father or mother more than me is not worthy of me: and he that loveth son or daughter more than me is not worthy of me (Matt. 10:37).

Many people have read that and wondered about it, and some

have turned away from it. But it is a very straightforward, dogmatic statement and it implies something big, something important. God is most important to any soul. Mark reports an incident that reveals this truth most vividly and as it appears in this incident it is more clearly understood.

> There came then his brethren and his mother, and, standing without, sent unto him, calling him. And the multitude sat about him, and they said unto him, Behold, thy mother and thy brethren without seek for thee. And he answered them, saying, Who is my mother, or my brethren? And he looked round about on them which sat about him, and said, Behold my mother and my brethren! For whosoever shall do the will of God, the same is my brother, and my sister, and mother (Mark 3:31-35).

In one sentence He set social relationships lower than spiritual relationships. Was He doing any violence to nature and to reality when He did that? Consider the nature of man: so far as the individual man is concerned, his self and what he thinks of himself, is the nearest to him. Because of his interest in self and because there would not be any man not interested in himself, it should lead him to want to be saved. The social group he is in gives him values: purposes, pleasures and riches in living. All these are grounded in the social group and are necessary to life and to happiness. Those things extend as far as the man can see or think or understand, but we know there is much more. All he sees will be in the social group – the people who are with him and who are against him; the people he works for and so on. But all he sees and thinks and understands, is limited within his range. The spiritual relationship, his relationship to God, Creator, Maker of the whole universe, includes and controls all things. Insofar as the human being is concerned the relationship with God is essential for his everlasting security and joy. If that human being, sensing himself as he is, knows that over all is God and his relationship with God is basically primary over everything, he will then experience eternal security.

What does any father, who really cares, want for his son? When I as a father think of this, I find I wanted my sons to have opportunity, to have protection. I wished for them help if they should get into real trouble, and should feel their own weakness, and I wished for them security. Who alone could provide and guarantee these but God? Who could in the last analysis give them security so they would be safe, if not God? And so, because I was interested in my sons, my relationship with God was more important than my immediate relationship with them.

Think of a mother and her child. The mother takes the child to the dentist, and he says the tooth will have to come out. The child says he does not want the tooth pulled. What is the mother going to do: is she going to be influenced by her son or is she going to go along with the dentist? If she has any sense at all she will agree with the dentist, for the boy's sake. Jesus of Nazareth was obedient. If I want to be His, what must I do? I too must be obedient to God. So when they came to Jesus of Nazareth and said, "Your mother and your brethren are without, asking for you," He taught them: "Look at these people listening to me. Look at these people who want to carry out my work, they are my mother and they are by brethren. These people come first in my own sense of values."

Chapter 20

PARABLE OF THE SOWER

(Mark 4:1-20)

> All these things spake Jesus unto the multitude in parables; and without a parable spake he not unto them (Matt. 13:34).

That last clause is one that often recurs to me. At this point we should be clear in our minds what a parable is. In the Bible a parable is used as an actual illustration. When the word "parable" is used in the New Testament we can have in mind that we are thinking about what we ordinarily call an illustration: usually a story told to convey an idea. It sets up a pattern of truth and when we are trying to say, for example, that the preaching of the gospel is important to believing people it is like saying that drinking milk is important to a child. That illustrated what we had in mind.

Jesus of Nazareth came to teach the truth about God, about His gospel, about heaven, about eternal life, and various aspects of the spiritual world. The spiritual world is invisible to us. It is infinite and eternal. It goes far beyond us. Then how can the truth about the spiritual world be shared? Obviously by the use of illustration. Paul said the invisible things of God are clearly seen by the things that are made, even His eternal power and Godhead. And so we look into events of earth, illustrations in nature and in experience, and we use those. It is common for us to speak of heaven as our home; we think of God as our Father, and ourselves as His children. We speak of believers as being brothers with each other. We speak of the church being the body of Christ, and the members of the church being members of the body. These are all figures of speech that convey truth.

> And he began again to teach by the seaside: and there was gathered unto him a great multitude, so that he entered into a ship, and sat in the sea; and the whole multitude was by the sea on the land. And he taught them many things by parables, and said unto them in his doctrine, Hearken;

> Behold, there went out a sower to sow: and it came to pass, as he sowed, some fell by the wayside, and the fowls of the air came and devoured it up. And some fell on stony ground, where it had not much earth; and immediately it sprang up, because it had no depth of earth: but when the sun was up, it was scorched; and because it had no root, it withered away. And some fell among thorns, and the thorns grew up, and choked it, and it yielded no fruit. And other fell on good ground, and did yield fruit that sprang up and increased; and brought forth, some thirty, and some sixty, and some a hundred. And he said unto them, He that hath ears to hear, let him hear (Mark 4:1-9).

This is commonly called the Parable of the Sower. You will not need to look at it too closely to see that it really could more properly be called "the Parable of the Soils" since it is actually about four kinds of soil. This parable is based on farming, but it is not told to guide the farmer; it is used to teach something to us all.

> And he said unto them, Unto you it is given to know the mystery of the kingdom of God: but unto them that are without, all these things are done in parables: that seeing they may see, and not perceive; and hearing they may hear, and not understand; lest at any time they should be converted, and their sins should be forgiven them (Mark 4:11-12).

This is both illuminating and drastic. "Unto you (the believers) it is given to know the mystery (and that in Greek is simple enough – the hidden things) of the kingdom of God: but unto them that are without (the people who have no faith) all these things are done in parables" (they are done by way of illustration). The twelfth verse is a rather literal translation of a difficult Old Testament passage.

> And he said, (God speaking to Isaiah) Go, and tell this people, Hear ye indeed, but understand not; and see ye indeed, but perceive not. Make the heart of this people fat, and make their ears heavy, and shut their eyes; lest they see with their eyes, and hear with their ears, and understand with their heart, and convert, and be healed (Isa. 6:9-10).

The way this is translated into English one would think God was going to act to hurt them, but in the Hebrew the idea is that they make their hearts fat, their ears heavy and they shut their eyes for this reason: they do not want to see lest they see with their eyes and hear with their ears and understand with their heart and convert and be healed, and they don't want that. In explaining to His disciples He is saying there are many people who are willfully set in such an attitude of mind, spiritual matters are invisible to them. They have shut off their minds.

So He sets the pattern in an illustration that can be interpreted by anyone who is willing and everyone else has to admit the illustration was all right.

We have here the case of the sower who went forth to sow. Everyone knows about that; we have even seen pictures of it. It may be that you have not shared in that kind of sowing, when you would go out with a bag under your arms with grain to be sowed. You would take the grain in your hand, and swinging your arm around throw out the seed, scattering it wherever it falls. I can remember days when I have seen that done. I have seen my father sow grass seed in a field, walking along and swinging his arm around and scattering it by hand. Some of the seeds fall upon a path. Suppose those grains of wheat fell on the pathway – what would happen? They would lie there until the birds would come and pick them. Although that was good seed, it did not produce anything. It never did get into the soil. That's one kind of soil.

Then there is the stony ground – soil that is shallow with stones in it. The stones would attract the heat of the sun, so the seed would germinate quickly and spring up fast. But when the weather would get hotter the soil would dry out and because the grain had no roots it withered; and of course there was no crop.

Then there is some soil that is good, rich land but weedy. The seed falls among the thorns. It will grow but it will never produce fruit because the weeds choke it out. Some falls into good ground and comes up with varying results – some thirtyfold, some sixty, and some a hundred.

This parable needed to be interpreted:

> And he said unto them, Know ye not this parable? and how then will ye know all parables? The sower soweth the word [that's the gospel spread out]. And these are they by the wayside, where the word is sown; but when they have heard, Satan cometh immediately, and taketh away the word that was sown in their hearts. [These are the people who don't understand it or accept it; they hear it but don't pay any attention to it.] And these are they likewise which are sown on stony ground; who, when they have heard the word, immediately receive it with gladness; and have no root in themselves, and so endure but for a time: afterward, when affliction or persecution ariseth for the word's sake, immediately they are offended. And these are they which are sown among thorns; such as hear the word, and the cares of this world, and the deceitfulness of riches, and the lusts of other things entering in, choke the word, and it becometh unfruitful. And these are they which are sown on good ground; such as hear the word, and receive it, and bring forth fruit, some thirtyfold, some sixty, and some a hundred (Mark 4:13-20, bracketed commentary mine).

What truth is being illustrated? The same gospel will produce different results in different people, but this is not the fault of the gospel or even, for that matter, to the credit of the gospel; the gospel does not do it. The gospel would produce fruit in any case if it were properly received. It is the heart of the person, the attitude and the frame of mind, that causes the different results in the spread of the gospel. This is what the Lord is showing in this parable. He is helping His disciples to realize that when they teach and preach they will have people at different levels listening to them. Some of the people will be thoroughly sincere and they will be greatly blessed. Some of the people would understand it and be blessed but they have too many things to do. The cares of this world, the deceitfulness of riches and the pleasures of this world enter in and crowd it out and it becomes unfruitful. Then there are those who receive it and think they understand it. They go forth and the first time they have trouble about it, they quit. Then there are some who do not pay any attention at all. They just don't care. They hear it and drop it; and of course, it won't stay with them. The enemy will come and get it out of their minds at once. That's the way it happens: always the same gospel, always the possibility of salvation: some will receive it and some will not. This is the truth which the Lord taught His disciples.

Chapter 21

PARABLES OF THE KINGDOM

(Mark 4:21-32)

> For the invisible things of him from the creation of the world are clearly seen, being understood by the things that are made, even his eternal power and Godhead; so that they are without excuse (Rom. 1:20).

To be sure, we have wonderful things to tell about, wonderful promises to share, when we set forth the gospel. When the wonders of His grace are told we are inclined to think the spiritual world must be magic, but this is not true. There is one exceptional thing, and that is God's action in grace giving His Son for my sins and raising me from the dead in Him. That was His idea and it comes from Him. It is not something that happened in the course of events. This originated in heaven, where He made up His mind, and so far as His conduct is concerned, it was spontaneous, an act of His own free will. But what takes place in this world, in the case of a believer, follows the established pattern in the world of nature.

One can learn about spiritual happenings by observing natural happenings. I will give you an example: in the natural world, to grow a plant you must have seed, and in the spiritual world, to have a saved soul there must be faith. If there is no faith in the individual no soul is going to be saved. "Without faith it is impossible to please him" (Heb. 11:6). You cannot just snap your finger and have faith. A person doesn't just say, "Well, I am going to believe." I would ask: "What are you going to believe? In whom are you going to believe?" If you don't know the promises of God you can't believe them, can you? Faith cometh by hearing and hearing by the Word of God. Paul said that whosoever shall call upon the name of the Lord shall be saved, and that is true! But:

> How then shall they call on him in whom they have not believed? and how shall they believe in him of whom they have not heard? (Rom. 10:14).

Faith cometh by hearing and hearing by the Word of God,

which is the seed. When it is heard and received it brings forth fruit and the fruit that it brings forth is faith. Faith leads on into salvation. That is the wonder of it.

> And he said, So is the kingdom of God, as if a man should cast seed into the ground; and should sleep, and rise night and day, and the seed should spring and grow up, he knoweth not how. For the earth bringeth forth fruit of herself; first the blade, then the ear, after that the full corn in the ear. But when the fruit is brought forth, immediately he putteth in the sickle, because the harvest is come (Mark 4:26-29).

Some years ago we had a garden, and I worked hard to make the plants grow. I can remember how astonishing it was to me after I had worked in the garden all week, then did not work on Saturday or Sunday, to look in the garden on Monday and find that the plants had grown over the weekend. I had paid no attention to them for two days, yet they grew. The Lord causes these things to happen. "If a man should cast seed into the ground; and should sleep, and rise night and day, (go on about his personal routine affairs) and the seed should spring and grow up, he knoweth not how." (You can't tell by looking at it; it is amazing that the plant should grow up out of that ground.) "For the earth bringeth forth fruit of herself, first the blade, then the ear, after that the full corn in the ear." I emphasize this because it is not written to tell us about farming but to tell us about spiritual matters. He wants to tell us that once the Word of God is heard it begins to grow. Silently, invisibly, unconsciously, during routine living. First the blade, then the ear, then the full corn in the ear. It takes time and it passes through stages in a normal way. When the growing, developing process reaches the stage of action and obedience, there comes a time of decisive action.

The Lord said in His parable, "he putteth in the sickle, because the harvest is come." That process is over and this is the parable He told to bring to our minds the truth that so far as producing the results of the gospel, so far as producing faith in the hearers so that they can believe and be saved, you and I who witness, who tell the story, who repeat it to other people, have nothing to do with what happens inside the heart. I am sure many of you are hoping and praying unto God that this might be true in your case. Wouldn't you be glad to think that having had your children memorize verses in the Bible, and having acquainted them with various stories in the Bible, the gospel would grow in their hearts and one day decisive action would be taken? We know that if we bring up our children in the way they should go when they are old they will not depart from it.

These promises are precious and you and I know they are true. It does not work in every case, it is possible the child did not hear in every case. You remember the parable of the soil that was hard because it was by the wayside? The seed that fell on that path never did enter into the ground, and the birds of the air came and carried it away. That can happen to people although it is not for us to know. It is for us to scatter the seed in prayerful fashion.

> And he said, Whereunto shall we liken the kingdom of God? or with what comparison shall we compare it? It is like a grain of mustard seed, which, when it is sown in the earth, is less than all the seeds that be in the earth: but when it is sown, it groweth up, and becometh greater than all herbs, and shooteth out great branches; so that the fowls of the air may lodge under the shadow of it (Mark 4:30-32).

Most of us are not well acquainted with the mustard plant. Even the mustard plant we have in this country is probably not quite the same as the plant that grew in the Orient. We do know some things: the seeds themselves are very small black seeds. They look just like dots on a page (they are that small), and the plant is quite tall, from one to three feet high. Those of us who have worked in the wheat fields in our boyhood days pulling mustard – we know about mustard. These plants grow tall in this country – it is possible they grew even taller in Palestine. They were described as being so tall the birds of the air were able to lodge under the shadow of them. The point He is making is that from such a little thing – such a little seed – this big plant will grow.

He told that parable for us to learn something from it. The parable shows the extraordinary vitality of the gospel. The mustard plants growing from such a tiny seed becomes the size of a shrub; this demonstrates how so little of the gospel becomes so much in experience in life. The gospel is so powerful one verse of Scripture can bring about regeneration. The story of Christ dying on the cross for sinners can be simply told, but it can regenerate souls. Christianity is the greatest example of amazing growth in history. Beginning in a small obscure province in the Roman Empire among a few people it has spread to where it covers the whole earth. Consider the power of the gospel in biography, and how a man like Saul the Pharisee, dead set against the gospel, became Paul the apostle. All of this should bring to our minds that we should never underestimate the power of the gospel.

Chapter 22

STILLING THE STORM

(Mark 4:33-41)

In the last chapter we noticed how Jesus of Nazareth taught His disciples about the ways of the spiritual world, the ways of the Spirit of God. We found that spiritual events occur as natural events in an even flow of logical, sequential relationships. All of that is true, but that is not all. The ways of God may follow a natural pattern like the growing of a plant: first the seed, then the blade, then the ear, then the full corn in the ear. But the power of God is supernatural. It is not contrary to nature, nor is it anti-natural; it is not against nature, but it is supernatural. The description of the ways of God, the processes involved in any operation of His, can be described as we have just said: first, the blade, then the ear, then the full corn in the ear; but the demonstration of the power of God, the activation of the will of God, must be done in events. There is no way to describe that. It is not an explosion or a great push; it is just something that happens and needs to be shown that way.

> And the same day, when the even was come, he saith unto them, Let us pass over unto the other side. And when they had sent away the multitude, they took him even as he was in the ship. And there were also with him other little ships. And there arose a great storm of wind, and the waves beat into the ship, so that it was now full. And he was in the hinder part of the ship, asleep on a pillow: and they awake him, and say unto him, Master, carest thou not that we perish? And he arose, and rebuked the wind, and said unto the sea, Peace, be still. And the wind ceased, and there was a great calm. And he said unto them, Why are ye so fearful? how is it that ye have no faith? And they feared exceedingly, and said one to another, What manner of man is this, that even the wind and the sea obey him? (Mark 4:35-41).

Let me make a comment here: a storm always seems so unnecessary. In our country there are the land, the valleys, hills, trees, sky and flowers. It is peaceful and the sun is shining; then a storm arises. There are those of us who have made a study of these natural processes. We can offer explanations, as the weatherman does, about how it happens, but so far as we are concerned it seems almost without any reason. Natural forces work together to create a dangerous situation, threatening to destroy, and whatever is true out in the country is far worse at sea. There the wind whips the ocean into high mountainous waves that threaten a ship; and that is a storm. When we read, "There arose a great storm of wind," all who have been on a boat will know that gusts of wind can arise and this happens.

The incident seems quite ordinary but there is a message here for us. No special circumstances are noted. It did not happen on a certain day in the week under certain conditions, nor did the storm come because someone did something. The storm became so threatening that the people were in danger. Jesus of Nazareth was in the back of the ship asleep on a pillow. We should note several things: He was with them when this crisis developed. Having the presence of the Lord did not stop the storm from coming. He did not take any steps to stop the storm until He was asked. We may also observe it seems strange that He should be asleep, although it was at evening time when they went on the boat. He was probably quite tired. Notice this: a storm may develop that presents a problem beyond our control or power to withstand, even though the Lord is in our midst. Circumstances may suddenly become violent and threatening and perilous even though we know right well we believe in the Lord, and we are counting on Him to be with us.

The statement that the Lord was asleep brings to our minds the truth that storms can arise at a time when it looks as though the Lord is not doing anything about it. In this case they awakened Him and that implies they had faith in Him. However, they did not call on Him until they were in extremity; and how often that is true about us. When they did call upon Him, this is what they said: "Master, carest thou not that we perish?" One can almost feel the element of rebuke here as if they were challenging His faithfulness. How easy it is for us to feel that way when trouble comes. "Why did You let this happen? Why is this coming to me? Have You turned Your back on me?" They were ready to blame Him; like children they had counted on Him. They believed He *could* and they were disturbed because He had not done anything. How common this is with all of us: we know God can and we are inclined to be almost pathetically petulant when He doesn't take action we can see. In this instance the disciples forgot they had not asked before.

And he arose, and rebuked the wind, and said unto the sea,

> Peace, be still. And the wind ceased, and there was a great calm (Mark 4:39).

He spoke the Word and all was quiet. He could have done that before but He did not: was it because He wanted them to ask? Did He want them actually to have that experience? He turned to them and asked: "Why are ye so fearful? how is it that ye have no faith?" Is this pointing out that they had gone along handling the boat and not really depending on Him until the wind became so bad they grew panicky and called Him? Isn't that a picture of how it often happens with us? No wonder their response was like this: "What manner of man is this, that even the wind and the sea obey him?" And that is what I think the Lord wants us to learn.

Do you have storms in your affairs? Is it possible that within your home there are occasional storms, or in your business? Have you ever been in a storm at sea? Have you ever had the feeling about what was happening to you in business, in the home, that you were suddenly helpless in a great storm? The feeling that everything has gone haywire? If that ever happens again you are to remember that He is able. There was demonstrated here God's great power to control the forces of nature. The forces of nature can bring us real trouble. Things around us in this world can bother us a great deal, but believers are to lift up their eyes beyond those things. They are to look up into the presence of God and know that He is greater than anything in this world. Eternity is longer than anything that can happen in time. We should not be terribly upset because of anything that might happen here. Things will never be perfect here in any case. Storms and disasters are going to occur; calamities will happen. "In the world you shall have tribulation." But the Lord said, "Be of good cheer, I have overcome the world."

In this incident we see Him overcoming the forces of nature. I am to remember that if He can do it out there in the storm at sea, He can do it in my heart and in my life, in your heart and in your life, and He can do it in our homes.

Chapter 23

HEALING OF THE GADARENE DEMONIAC

(Mark 5:1-20)

In Mark's Gospel we have noticed several incidents in which Jesus of Nazareth gave a description of the spiritual processes that are activated by the will of God. He told His disciples how things happen when God does them. The parables show how the operation of the power of God in spiritual matters is like the natural processes of cause-and-effect relationships in events. He taught them to understand that the ways of God in this world follow, first the seed, then the blade, then the ear, then the full corn in the ear. There is a sequence of events that is natural and that is normal, and, in a sense, logical.

We come now to a series of incidents in which the power of God is revealed in a more unusual manner. In the last chapter we noticed the stilling of the storm. All the processes of nature were active in that storm in a natural, normal way until the Lord commanded, "Peace, be still." Something then happened that was astonishing: God's power over nature was revealed. This showed how Jesus Christ, the Son of God, actually had power over natural events while He was here on earth. He had it then and He has it now. What we are about to see happen in the account which is written here in Mark, has no natural explanation; it is a demonstration of supernatural power.

> And they came over unto the other side of the sea, into the country of the Gadarenes. And when he was come out of the ship, immediately there met him out of the tombs a man with an unclean spirit (Mark 5:1-2).

This man was ostracized from society and was living in what we could call a graveyard, among the tombs carved out of the walls of the cliffs in that hilly country. When the New Testament refers to "unclean spirits" it is speaking of what we commonly call "demons."

The account goes on to relate:

> Who had his dwelling among the tombs; and no man could

> bind him, no, not with chains: because that he had been often bound with fetters and chains, and the chains had been plucked asunder by him, and the fetters broken in pieces: neither could any man tame him (Mark 5:3-4).

This man was so possessed by demons he gave exhibitions of abnormal strength because of being inwardly torn by this demon.

> And always, night and day, he was in the mountains, and in the tombs, crying, and cutting himself with stones (Mark 5:5).

Today we would say he was demented. His mind was not his own. Some would say he was "crazy," which means that nothing fits a pattern. He was a man so affected inwardly, psychically, that he acted with abnormal strength. The Bible simply says he was possessed with a demon.

How did the man get that way? This can be described as some kind of psychological aberration but all such descriptions are simply our own opinion. I would prefer the way Mark puts it, because I think it has aspects about it that are far more than can be explained as some aberration of the human personality. This is the case of a man who has been possessed by another mind than his own, another will than his own.

> But when he saw Jesus afar off, he ran and worshiped him, and cried with a loud voice, and said, What have I to do with thee, Jesus, thou Son of the most high God? I adjure thee by God, that thou torment me not. For he said unto him, Come out of the man, thou unclean spirit. And he asked him, What is thy name? And he answered, saying, My name is Legion: for we are many. And he besought him much that he would not send them away out of the country (Mark 5:6-10).

This demon asked the Lord not to send him away out of the country, why? I do not know. That requires an understanding of demon thinking I do not have.

> Now there was there nigh unto the mountains a great herd of swine feeding. And all the devils besought him, saying, Send us into the swine, that we may enter into them. And forthwith Jesus gave them leave. And the unclean spirits went out, and entered into the swine: and the herd ran violently down a steep place into the sea, (they were about two thousand;) and were choked in the sea. And they that fed the swine fled, and told it in the city, and in the country. And they went out to see what it was that was done. And they come to Jesus, and see him that was possessed with the devil, and had the legion, sitting, and clothed, and in his right mind: and they were afraid. And they that saw it told them how it befell to him that was possessed with the devil, and also concerning the swine. And they began to pray him to depart out of their coasts (Mark 5:11-17).

When these neighbors saw the evidence of the power of God in action, it frightened them and they wanted to go away. How blind can people be? Here was a demonstration of the power of God in which a man's soul was set free because the power of God was exercised against the demons that had held the man in their control, and when it actually happened before them, they asked Him to leave the country.

> And when he was come into the ship, he that had been possessed with the devil prayed him that he might be with him. Howbeit Jesus suffered him not, but saith unto him, Go home to thy friends, and tell them how great things the Lord hath done for thee, and hath had compassion on thee. And he departed, and began to publish in Decapolis how great things Jesus had done for him: and all men did marvel (Mark 5:18-20).

That's the story, eloquent in itself! It shows us a wonderful truth: the power of God in controlling the forces of evil, even demonic forces, is wonderful! But men can be so blind that they actually push the power away, as if they preferred to live on in darkness!

Chapter 24

HEALING OF JAIRUS' DAUGHTER

(Mark 5:21-24; 35-43)

We learn from the Scriptures that when Jesus of Nazareth moved about in the country preaching and teaching, sinners gathered around Him; now I wonder what we will say about the righteous? He said He didn't come to call the righteous but sinners to repentance, but how about the case of a man who himself is a good man – is he therefore shut out? There is something here all of us need to understand. A song has a line in it that says, "Whosoever, surely meaneth me." And that is the truth. Regardless of what level we may be on or what prestige we may have; whether we be high or low, far ahead or far behind, the message is to us. Mark has a way of emphasizing the marvelous truth that anyone may come, and he shows this in an incident we now note.

> And when Jesus was passed over again by ship unto the other side, much people gathered unto him: and he was nigh unto the sea. And, behold, there cometh one of the rulers of the synagogue, Jairus by name; and when he saw him, he fell at his feet, and besought him greatly, saying, My little daughter lieth at the point of death: I pray thee, come and lay thy hands on her, that she may be healed; and she shall live. And Jesus went with him; and much people followed him, and thronged him (Mark 5:21-24).

By this time people had begun to talk about Him, because there were a number of things He had done that drew attention, so a large crowd was on hand. Jairus was one of the leaders of the people, an important man. He came from a group of men who were usually opposed to Jesus of Nazareth. It is true the poor have the gospel preached unto them, and they could come; but not all poor people come. Even so not all rich people are left out: some poor come and some rich come. It may be that proportionately more poor than rich came, though the Bible does not tell us this. Being poor does not necessarily guarantee you will have the blessing of God, just as being rich does not guarantee you will be shut out from the blessing of God. We oftentimes say the gospel is for "the down and outers," and that is true; but the gospel is also for the "up and outers." We should never forget that.

One of the rulers of the synagogue came "and when he saw him, he fell at his feet." Take note of this humble attitude: it does not matter whether you are rich or poor, it is a matter of the heart. A humble and a contrite heart the Lord will not despise. A rich man may be humble and a poor man may also be humble. The rich may be proud but the poor may also be proud. And the pride of the poor is a difficult thing to handle.

> And besought him greatly, saying, My little daughter lieth at the point of death: I pray thee, come and lay thy hands on her, that she may be healed; and she shall live (Mark 5:23).

I want you to feel this man's faith. This is a parent praying for his child and I have this in my notes in the margin of my Bible: "Fathers, take note." A father may pray for his child; he does not have to leave it to the mother. If you do not know how to pray, you can pray in your heart and pray privately, but *pray* to God about your children. This reminds us of the leper who, when he came, said, "Lord, if thou wilt thou canst make me clean." The Lord had compassion on him: "I will, be thou clean"; and immediately his leprosy was cleansed.

It is a marvelous thing when you have faith to come into the presence of God and talk for your children. Talk for your son, young or old, and ask God for help.

> And Jesus went with him; and much people followed him, and thronged him . . . While he yet spake, there came from the ruler of the synagogue's house certain which said, Thy daughter is dead: why troublest thou the Master any further? [This was a natural frame of mind. They had been ministering to her and apparently she had died, so they told the father nothing more could be done.] As soon as Jesus heard the word that was spoken, he saith unto the ruler of the synagogue, Be not afraid, only believe. [This is an amazing thing. Isn't it too late? Apparently not. You are still alive, the Lord is still in heaven and you can talk to Him. Be not afraid, only believe.] And he suffered no man to follow him, save Peter, and James, and John the brother of James. And he cometh to the house of the ruler of the synagogue, and seeth the tumult, and them that wept and wailed greatly. And when he was come in, he saith unto them, Why make ye this ado, and weep? the damsel is not dead, but sleepeth. And they laughed him to scorn (Mark 5:24; 35-40, bracketed comments mine).

There are some demonstrations of the power of God reserved

for those close to the Lord. Would you like to have been Peter, James or John? They had no special qualifications as men; apparently they simply believed in the Lord and were close to Him. They did not always agree with everything He did. Peter often did not understand Him, but still he was earnest and sincere and followed Him.

The Lord would not let anyone come with Him when He was going to raise this girl except these three. When He announced the damsel was not dead but sleeping, the people laughed him to scorn. For me, and perhaps for you, if we had been laughed to scorn we would feel like running or quitting, but He didn't. Why not? He knew what He was going to do and that He did not need to run. At this point I have this in my notes: (This is the Lord, the Sovereign, and the Sovereign God is going to say, "This girl is only sleeping." He can wake her up.) All that I can do here is point you to the Lord and remind you that this record points directly to His authority. He will raise whom He will.

> But when he had put them all out, he taketh the father and the mother of the damsel, and them that were with him, and entereth in where the damsel was lying. And he took the damsel by the hand, and said unto her, Tal-i-tha cu-mi; which is, being interpreted, Damsel, (I say unto thee,) arise. And straightway the damsel arose and walked; for she was of the age of twelve years. And they were astonished with a great astonishment. And he charged them straitly that no man should know it; and commanded that something should be given her to eat (Mark 5:40-43).

Isn't that interesting? True, He had raised her from the dead, but she still needed to eat. Certainly God can do exceptional things, but the merely physical things count too. In this case He commanded that something should be given to her to eat.

Chapter 25

HEALING OF THE ISSUE OF BLOOD

(Mark 5:25-34)

Confidence in faith healing has been reported again and again in the history of the church. I know we hear much about it now, but the last generation heard about it then, and people fifty years ago and a hundred years ago heard about it then. All through the history of the church this has been coming up again and again, and this should be no surprise because when you read the New Testament you have it right there before you. Interest has always been high in this matter. Anyone who is ill would be glad to be made well, and this is one of the reasons why we are all concerned with any procedure that promises healing. We may not all be ill, but we may have loved ones who are ill, and we wonder if they can be healed. Almost everyone would be glad to see healings to the glory of the name of the Lord Jesus Christ.

Mark gives us an account of an unusual incident. Let us study this demonstration of the power of God.

> And a certain woman, which had an issue of blood twelve years, and had suffered many things of many physicians, and had spent all that she had, and was nothing bettered, but rather grew worse, when she had heard of Jesus, came in the press behind, and touched his garment. For she said, If I may touch but his clothes, I shall be whole. And straightway the fountain of her blood was dried up; and she felt in her body that she was healed of that plague. And Jesus, immediately knowing in himself that virtue had gone out of him, turned him about in the press, and said, Who touched my clothes? And his disciples said unto him, Thou seest the multitude thronging thee, and sayest thou, Who touched me? And he looked round about to see her that had done this thing. But the woman fearing and trembling, knowing what was done in her, came and fell down before him, and told him all the truth. And he said unto her, Daughter, thy faith hath made thee whole; go in peace, and be whole of thy plague (Mark 5:25-34).

Look at it more closely: "A certain woman had had an issue

of blood" (she had been hemorrhaging for twelve years). "Had suffered many things of many physicians, and had spent all that she had, and was nothing bettered, but rather grew worse." We have here a factual statement of just what had happened to this afflicted woman. Luke, who was a doctor, also tells the story but reports it a bit differently, "which had spent all her living upon physicians neither could be healed of any." Luke, the doctor, said she could not be healed; that she was incurable. Mark, the layman, said she had spent all she had and was nothing bettered but rather grew worse. He simply tells it from the point of view of the layman.

The woman had heard of Jesus of Nazareth. This seems to emphasize how important it is to talk about Him. How important it is to tell the unbelieving person about Jesus of Nazareth. She was not born with that knowledge, and she did not know about Him intuitively, nor did she know about Him by special revelation: there was no vision that came to her, or anything like that. When she had heard of Jesus of Nazareth it was because someone talked about Him.

Let us ask ourselves soberly: where could one hear about Him today? Would it be at the Sunday school? Then let us face this issue honestly: will they teach the children in the Sunday school that Jesus Christ can heal any person who comes to Him? Will they teach in the Sunday school that this woman who had been twelve years with a hemorrhage came, and touched Him and was healed? Think it over. Will your preacher preach it that way in the pulpit? Will he tell the people that Jesus Christ is able to heal by His power those who come unto Him? I am not going to say He will heal everyone. This woman was sick and she came to Him. Did the people who went to your church last Sunday hear that Jesus Christ can heal?

In many church services and young people's meetings and even in Sunday school, children do not hear that He can heal. We should never fail publicly to let it be known that so far as we are concerned we believe the living Lord Jesus Christ can heal if it suits His purpose. It probably will not suit His purpose to heal everyone. Some people will get sick and will die. "It is appointed unto man once to die." But should we leave the impression that here is any reason to doubt Jesus Christ could do these things?

When this woman heard of Jesus she came through the crowd and touched His garment. She said, "If I may touch but his clothes, I shall be whole." Her confidence was in the Lord. She believed He could heal her. She was in such a condition she needed it, and her action put the two together: she needed it and He could. "And straightway the fountain of her blood was dried up." The woman was healed. Some may say, "I don't believe it." Does that change anything? It only means that so far as one person is concerned, he does not expect anything. Those who do not expect anything from the Lord will not get anything from Him.

No one else had been able to heal this woman. She came to Him, trusted Him, and He healed her. "And Jesus, immediately knowing in himself that virtue had gone out of him, turned him about in the press, and said, Who touched my clothes?" Do you think He needed to ask for information? Do you think for one moment Jesus of Nazareth was in any doubt as to who it was? Then why did He ask it? Because of what followed. First of all, His disciples said unto Him, "Thou seest the multitude thronging thee, and sayest thou, Who touched me?" Such a question is ridiculous. "And he looked round about to see her that had done this thing." He had not taken time to answer them. He looked around immediately to see this woman. "But the woman fearing and trembling, knowing what was done in her, came and fell down before him, and told him all the truth. And he said unto her, Daughter, thy faith hath made thee whole; go in peace, and be whole of thy plague."

What can we learn here? What is actually shown to all of us in this account? Here is a humble person who has a persistent disease. Something is wrong inside her body, and for twelve years it has troubled her. It has cost her everything she had. Her faith in the Lord made her feel He could do something about it. She acted on that faith. Because she had faith, she crowded through the people, came to Him, and touched His clothing. "If I may touch but his clothes" and that is what she did. Immediately she was healed and she was blessed. That is the pattern for you and me. At all times we can know the living Jesus Christ is available, "able to save to the uttermost."

I do not know what your problem may be, but I want to tell you: the living Lord in heaven does know. If you will look up to Him and ask Him for help, to give you the grace to believe, I can assure you He can and will help you. I remember so well the words of my great teacher, Dr. R. A. Torrey, who once said about healing, that Christian people suffered far more pain and disease and physical trouble than they needed to. If they would just bring these things before the Lord in prayer many of them would be healed and helped by the power of God.

Chapter 26

UNBELIEF OF HIS NEIGHBORS

(Mark 6:1-6)

"Whosoever believeth in him should not perish, but have eternal life" (John 3:15). These familiar words lead us directly to the very heart of the gospel. What does it mean to believe in Jesus Christ? Would it be enough to admit there was such a person, that He was crucified, that He is the Head of the Church, founder of the Christian religion? No: all that but more is implied by these words. What does "calling upon the name of the Lord" mean? What does "unbelief" actually mean?

> And he went out from thence, and came into his own country; and his disciples follow him. And when the sabbath day was come, he began to teach in the synagogue: and many hearing him were astonished, saying, From whence hath this man these things? and what wisdom is this which is given unto him, that even such mighty works are wrought by his hands? Is not this the carpenter, the son of Mary, the brother of James, and Joses, and of Judah, and Simon? and are not his sisters here with us? And they were offended at him. But Jesus said unto them, A prophet is not without honor, but in his own country, and among his own kin, and in his own house. And he could there do no mighty work, save that he laid his hands upon a few sick folk, and healed them. And he marveled because of their unbelief. And he went round about the villages, teaching (Mark 6:1-6).

This is an actual case of unbelief. It meant not only that these people were without blessing, but it meant also that they actually hindered the work of the Lord among them. "He could there do no mighty work because of their unbelief." We are told He came into His own country, which was the region of Galilee, where He grew to manhood. "And when the sabbath day was come" (it was His custom on the Sabbath to go to the synagogue) "he began to teach in the synagogue."

What do you suppose He taught? No doubt this would refer to such instruction as we read in the four Gospels, particularly the Sermon on the Mount which is the compendium of what

He was teaching. He taught them the real meaning of the law. This was not to be found in the external regulations which had been developed by the teachers and thinkers among the Jewish people, and which constituted the requirements commonly held by the people. The real meaning of the law was deep, personal, spiritual, from the heart; and this is what is revealed in the Sermon on the Mount (Matthew 5, 6, 7). He also taught the promise of salvation to all who obey God, not only in the Sermon on the Mount, but as He moved among people. He taught them by parables how God does things. He taught them they needed to believe in God and on His Son; to trust Christ as Savior and Lord. Eventually He taught them to receive the Holy Spirit as Comforter, Companion and Guide.

He had not done all this early in His ministry but He did before He was through, and when we are thinking about the teaching of the Lord Jesus Christ this would be the kind of thing He was doing. He taught them by word – as when He set forth the parables. In using parables He was describing the processes of the work of God. What is it like when God works in a person? It is like the growing of a plant – first the blade, then the ear, then the full corn in the ear. This is the process of God as it is seen in this world. He also taught them by works – as in healing; because, as we pointed out, the way God does things may follow the way of the natural process but actually the power God exercises is an original thing. It is new, as in healing, when we have the case of the demons being cast out, inner sickness being cured, and deliverance from the influences of the evil one. When teaching in the synagogue He talked about the law, about believing in God. He talked about the way God worked things as He taught in parables. Every now and again He performed some miracle as, for instance, healing the man with the withered hand and other such instances in which He would demonstrate to the people what God would actually do. "Many hearing him were astonished." (They were amazed.) "From whence hath this man these things?" You will remember that as He was teaching He was not as the scribes but He taught them as one having authority, as if He could do what He was talking about, and did. "And what wisdom is this which is given unto him, that even such mighty works are wrought by his hands?" That was part of His teaching ministry; part of what He was showing forth. He was getting things done as human beings were brought, and listened to Him under the power of God. "Is not this the carpenter, the son of Mary, the brother of James, and Joses, and of Judah, and Simon? and are not his sisters here with us?"

Nowhere in the New Testament is Jesus of Nazareth referred to as the carpenter except here, by people who were unbelievers. If you are prone to refer to Him as "the man of Galilee" or as "the carpenter of Galilee," don't do it. You are not honoring Him in either case. The only people in those days who referred to Him in that manner were unbelievers. He is Christ Jesus. Give Him His name and His honor, the Lord Jesus Christ. "And they were offended at him." When this word "offended" is used here it does not mean they were emotionally disturbed; it means they were confused because they stumbled at all He represented. It was all so incredible! When He realized the attitude of His neighbors, He made this comment: "A prophet is not without honor, but in his own country, and among his own kin, and in his own house." Nothing further is said about that except this stern and awful word, "And he could there do no mighty work, save that he laid his hands upon a few sick folk, and healed them."

We normally would think that if He healed a sick person this action would be a mighty work. But this is not the attitude revealed in the New Testament. "He could there do no mighty work, save that he laid his hands upon a few sick folk, and healed them." Can you understand why the healing of the body is a lesser thing? The body is only for the time being – for a little while. The mighty work would have to do with changing a man's soul, changing his relationship with God. Then comes this sentence: "And he marveled because of their unbelief." What was that unbelief about? Was it that they did not believe Jesus of Nazareth was there? Certainly they believed that. Was it that they did not think His life on earth was real? They knew Him and they knew His brothers and sisters. No, that is not what unbelief means.

If someone were to say to me, "I believe that Jesus of Nazareth lived." Would he be saying anything much? "I believe that He died on the cross." So did hundreds and thousands of people in Jerusalem. They believed but it did not make them "believers"; it did not unite them with God. Someone might say, "I believe He died for sinners." That is true but it does not mean much for salvation. Let me ask you: "Did He die for you?" If He did not die for you it does not count. The devils know He died on the cross. What did He offer Himself to be? The sacrifice for sins, Head of the body, the indwelling Son of God, the Mediator between God and man. Why did they not believe in Him as the Son of God? Because they were preoccupied with His human form. So we ask ourselves: "Why could He not do there any mighty works?" Because they thought about Him as a man.

Chapter 27

SENDING OF HIS DISCIPLES

(Mark 6:7-13)

> For after that in the wisdom of God the world by wisdom [and this word wisdom in the Greek means philosophy — by rationalization] knew not God, it pleased God by the foolishness of preaching to save them that believe (1 Cor. 1:21, bracketed comments mine).

In that passage Paul makes the statement that the preaching of the Cross is to the Jews a stumbling block, and to the Greeks it is foolishness. But it was the will of God that the gospel of the Cross should be preached "to save them that believe." Here it is to be remembered that no man by searching can find out God. I wish this were known to all people. It is surprising how many people seem to agree with themselves to stay in the ranks of the unbelievers, saying, "I tried to find out and I couldn't find out. I have tried to understand and I couldn't understand." People will alibi in various ways by saying they were looking and looking, and could not see anything. We are reminded in Scripture: "Verily thou art a God that hidest thyself." But He can reveal Himself, and this He did in His Son, Jesus Christ, as set forth in the gospel.

We have to come to an understanding of the whole matter something like this: a person does not come to God by himself; he does not figure things out by himself. He does not review all he knows and so come to the conclusion that he knows God. Perhaps he could get to the place where he might think there must be a God but he still would not know Him. Coming to know God is not necessarily through personal face-to-face encounter. For instance, a person might read a book and come to God that way, but he would not come to God because it is good literature or because it has a fine argument. If the book presented truth about the Lord Jesus Christ, it could be possible. Things about the gospel of the Lord Jesus Christ can be contained in a book and often are. There are many books the reading of which would lead the heart and soul toward God.

This can also be done by means of gospel music. Just music itself, the ordinary flow of notes, would not have any spiritual power. The notes might have artistic power or they might have esthetic appeal. Some tunes are meaningful, but that is because we know the words that go with them; and it is the words that come to mind when the tune is sung. Songs, psalms, hymns, spiritual songs, all such may be helpful. There are also pictures that can bring certain aspects of gospel truth to mind. Various media may be used, but when you come right down to it, the basic media that will be used is words. It is basically a matter of telling it.

When Jesus of Nazareth came into this world, after John the Baptist had pointed Him out, two of John's disciples went to be with Him. Then we read that Andrew "first findeth his own brother Simon, and saith unto him, We have found the Messiah, which is, being interpreted, the Christ" (John 1:41). So the person goes out and tells it. The entire gospel account begins with statements like this. "There was a man sent from God, whose name was John." It belongs to the mercy and grace of God that He impels messengers to go out and tell. "Go ye into all the world and tell (and in one place) . . . and preach."

Having this in mind let us now look at what Mark records:

> And he called unto him the twelve, and began to send them forth by two and two; and gave them power over unclean spirits; and commanded them that they should take nothing for their journey, save a staff only; no scrip, no bread, no money in their purse: but be shod with sandals; and not put on two coats. And he said unto them, In what place soever ye enter into an house, there abide till ye depart from that place. And whosoever shall not receive you, nor hear you, when ye depart thence, shake off the dust under your feet for a testimony against them. Verily I say unto you, It shall be more tolerable for Sodom and Gomorrah in the day of judgment, than for that city. And they went out, and preached that men should repent. And they cast out many devils, and anointed with oil many that were sick, and healed them (Mark 6:7-13).

This is the story, short and compact, of how Jesus of Nazareth called His apostles and sent them forth. This is what is going on even to this day. God sends out His servants. Jesus of Nazareth told His disciples the fields are white unto harvest, "the harvest truly is plenteous, but the laborers are few; pray ye therefore the Lord of the harvest, that he will send forth laborers into his harvest." I think the actual translation may be thrust forth, for the Greek has in it the idea of pushing them – thrusting them forth – that they should do this.

So let us read this passage verse by verse and learn for ourselves: "And he called unto him the twelve, and began to send them forth by two and two; and gave them power over unclean spirits." These unclean spirits were outside influences. Many are dominated by the community in which they live, and by the people with whom they live, and by the ideas that prevail in the society in which they take part. Some of these ideas are not godly. Some unclean things may have control, and they can lead a person away from God. A person may be so enamored with things around him that he can be led away from God. One of the works these preachers were to do was to set the people free from the unclean spirits. Souls of men, generally speaking, are in bondage to the person of darkness far more than we may realize; and they may need to be released and delivered from this bondage. Souls may be so released by the power of God. This will involve their dying and being raised from the dead. This is only possible by the power of God, who will first find "the strong man" and then set the prisoner free.

What would such power be? There are various manifestations of power. One can think of power when a sledge hammer hits a post, or one may think of power as a magnet attracting iron. But one may also think of the power in a growing plant, the opening of a blossom, that does not come from anything except a seed. Something pushes it out and makes it open. When we talk about the power of God all these aspects may be involved. The main thing is that deliverance from bondage is not by reasoning, not by philosophy, not by argument, but by telling what God will do. God gave the apostles power over unclean spirits.

Jesus of Nazareth commanded them that they should take nothing for their journey save only a staff; no scrip (money), no bread. They were to be shod with sandals and have only one coat. They should be dependent upon the providence of God. The culture of the Jews assigned a definite responsibility on the part of the people for those among them who taught the Word of God. The instructions given by Jesus of Nazareth to His apostles would not cover the way they would be sent among Gentiles or among unbelieving people. This was the way they were sent among believing people: they were to be dependent upon God through His people. "And he said unto them, In what place soever ye enter into an house, there abide till ye depart from that place." (No shopping around: when you get rooted some place, go to work there.) "And whosoever shall not receive you, nor hear you, when ye depart thence, shake off the dust under your feet." (Those who reject this message of the gospel were to be referred to God.)

"And they went out, and preached that men should repent." Believing men should repent. People who belong to God should repent. Anyone who is worshiping God should repent. The person who comes into the presence of God should come in on this ground floor: "I am a sinner, I have done wrong. I need the grace of God." But this is only the introduction to the gospel; that is not our gospel. To become aware of sin and of sinfulness is the first step, to be sure, but this does not yet have saving power. These messengers were sent only to the house of Israel, not to the Gentiles. They preached that men should repent: which is like saying, "Empty your pails because I have something to give you."

"And they cast out many devils, (delivered many people from bondage) and anointed with oil many that were sick, and healed them." When we look at that record our hearts are stirred and challenged. Oh, how we could pray to God that such powerful testimony might take place amongst us! Let us keep in mind that the desire within our hearts to try to win other people is something that comes from God. And may His name be praised.

Chapter 28

DEATH OF JOHN THE BAPTIST

(Mark 6:14-29)

We are told John the Baptist was filled with the Holy Spirit from his youth. He would, therefore, be highly sensitive to spiritual matters; vitally aware of what was involved at any time in anything relating to the presence of God. He was a powerful preacher although he was only about thirty years of age. We read about him that all Jerusalem and Judah came to hear him. Mark tells the story of his tragic death, after recording what Herod thought when he heard of Jesus of Nazareth:

> And king Herod heard of him; (for his name was spread abroad:) and he said, That John the Baptist was risen from the dead, and therefore mighty works do show forth themselves in him (Mark 6:14).

Although the record speaks of Jesus of Nazareth and refers to John the Baptist as a preacher, what Herod particularly noticed were the mighty works that were done.

> Others said, That it is Elijah. And others said, That it is a prophet, or as one of the prophets. But when Herod heard thereof, he said, It is John, whom I beheaded: he is risen from the dead (Mark 6:15-16).

This shows the sudden fame of Jesus of Nazareth. It also shows how King Herod felt. Surprisingly, Herod was able and willing to believe in the resurrection from the dead. He was able to say, "It is John, whom I beheaded. And he has risen from the dead." I do not think this means that Herod had any idea at all about being raised from the dead in the way believers have in mind being raised from the dead through the power of the Lord Jesus Christ. When believers talk about being raised from the dead they do not expect ever to die again. They expect to be changed. But when Herod spoke about John being raised from the dead he may have thought of him in the way Lazarus was raised from the dead: a matter of being brought back to this life. This would mean for John a sort of re-run of his life: he would die again.

As the story unfolds there is further suggestion as to why Herod felt as he did. His conscience may have bothered him; but there was more involved.

> For Herod himself had sent forth and laid hold upon John, and bound him in prison for Herodias' sake, his brother Philip's wife: for he had married her. For John had said unto Herod, It is not lawful for thee to have thy brother's wife (Mark 6:17-18).

Herod had jailed John, not because he thought John was not a good man, and not because he was not impressed with John, but because John would not condone his personal conduct in marrying this woman. Herod actually appreciated John but he was socially influenced by the woman. "Therefore Herodias had a quarrel against him, and would have killed him; but she could not" (Mark 6:19). Herodias actually wanted to put John to death earlier, but she was not able to get away with it. She was malicious because John had criticized Herod for marrying her. "For Herod feared John," (the word "feared" implies more than just being scared as we would say in our ordinary speech. Herod did not think John would do him harm; he "feared" him with a sense of respect) "knowing that he was just a man and an holy, and observed him; and when he heard him, he did many things, and heard him gladly" (Mark 6:19-20).

Herod was actually affected by John's preaching and this is important for us to notice here. We come across this truth in several other places in the New Testament. Herod did not want to harm John yet he put him in prison! He acted in this way because of the influence of other people. This is not the first time it has happened that someone, influenced by others, has done harm to a man who has been faithful to the gospel.

> And when a convenient day was come, that Herod on his birthday made a supper to his lords, high captains, and chief estates of Galilee; and when the daughter of the said Herodias came in, and danced, and pleased Herod and them that sat with him, the king said unto the damsel, Ask of me whatsoever thou wilt, and I will give it thee. And he sware unto her, Whatsoever thou shalt ask of me, I will give it thee, unto the half of my kingdom. And she went forth, and said unto her mother, What shall I ask? And she said, The head of John the Baptist. And she came in straightway with haste unto the king, and asked, saying, I will that thou give me by and by in a charger the head of John the Baptist. And the king was exceeding sorry; yet for his oath's sake, and for their sakes which sat with him, he would not reject her. And immediately the king sent an executioner, and commanded his head to be brought: and he went and beheaded him in the prison, and brought his

> head in a charger, and gave it to the damsel: and the damsel gave it to her mother (Mark 6:21-28).

Such is the tragic story of the death of John the Baptist. Is it not strange that this man, the king, committed murder because he would not break his word? In this whole story the one person who stands out head and shoulders over everyone else is John the Baptist. Of all the things that happened there that day, the one person who was unblemished and whose testimony was really strong altogether was John the Baptist.

"And when his disciples heard of it, they came and took up his corpse, and laid it in a tomb" (Mark 6:29). It is obvious in reading this account that this tragic event was totally unnecessary, as all acts of violence are. Herod did not want to do this any more than Pilate wanted to give Jesus of Nazareth over to be crucified. It is dangerous for any human being to be so involved with other people that they can influence him to do something wrong. We all need to take this closely to heart: if you and I want to live an open, straightforward life we must be willing to break with others, because we fear God. It was this sort of situation that resulted in the death of John; and it can happen in a congregation. A good pastor can actually be smeared and "given over to the wolves" because of the influence of others. A speaker who is faithful in testifying to the truth will arouse harmful opposition. But it is a wonderful thing to know that God can overrule and make even the wrath of man to praise Him. The testimony of John the Baptist was "a burning and a shining light."

Chapter 29

DEPARTING INTO PRIVACY

(Mark 6:30-32)

Part of the practical problem of obeying God is due to our human limitations. We are personally weak; we wear out so easily. In one place Paul says we have this treasure in earthen vessels and oftentimes we feel we are truly made of clay. There is always the danger that a zealous servant committed to obey God will go beyond his human strength. That is always possible, and it happens many times. Mark records an action of the Lord we want to study because it will give us an insight into what should be done by anyone who is serving and obeying the Lord. We recently noted how the Lord commissioned and empowered His disciples to preach, to cast out demons, to heal the sick and to make known what the Lord could do. Now I want you to notice what happened after that.

> And the apostles gathered themselves together unto Jesus, and told him all things, both what they had done, and what they had taught. And he said unto them, Come ye yourselves apart into a desert place, and rest a while: for there were many coming and going, and they had no leisure so much as to eat. And they departed into a desert place by ship privately (Mark 6:30-32).

The apostles had been sent to preach and heal. Now they reported what they had done and I am sure it was a stirring meeting. Can you imagine all the things they had to tell – of their excitement to see the things that had happened? But then, there was no leisure and for that reason the Lord suggested they come apart into a desert place to rest. A desert place does not necessarily mean it was all sand and gravel and rocks, but it does mean it was a region uninhabited and quiet.

When you think about the matter of serving the Lord, or when you are wondering about doing His will, how would you know what God wanted you to do? How would you ever know whether He wanted you to go or to stay? You would know this only as you are led by Him, and that is an inner experience. It requires a personal exclusive line of communication between the human heart and God, through the Lord Jesus Christ. Were the disciples so weary they needed to rest? The record does not say. Were they so satisfied with what had been done that they did not care whether they did any more work or not? The record does not say. All we know is that they came back and reported to their Lord. They were ready to do as their Lord would lead them.

How does the Lord lead any of us? Sometimes by verbal utterance; we do not necessarily hear His actual voice, but perhaps He speaks through one of His servants. It may be some servant will make a statement, and that very statement rings in our hearts, and we know what He wants us to do. It is possible to feel at once what the Lord wants from me. Always I need to humble myself before God, and ask Him to give me the grace to accept His message for me.

Sometimes leading will come through the group with whom I am having fellowship. I might belong to a Sunday school class. That class may be supervised by a superintendent who asks me to do a particular task. Thus I get my direction. It may be that in my church as a whole there are certain things done by elders and deacons or by the pastor; and if the call to me to perform that task is according to the agreement that everyone accepts and is according to the constitution of the church, then it is for me a "structured direction." It may be that I will not receive any word specially spoken to me personally; or it may be I will receive direction from someone who lets me know he wants me to do a certain thing – perhaps teach Sunday school, or usher in the church. If the person speaking to me is an officer and is authorized to do this, I should be willing to accept his word as something that God wants me to do.

Paul said "the powers that be are ordained of God" (Rom. 13:1), and he implies that if I receive instruction the thing for me to do is to act according to what I receive. So this could be the way the Lord would lead. Sometimes the Lord will lead in providence, when things just seem to work out that way. A case in point: if I were wondering how to get downtown, and someone came by and offered me a ride, I could accept this as from the Lord.

We read in the next verse: "And they departed into a desert place by ship privately." Was the public willing to let them go? That is not the point. They did not go because people wanted them to go; they were led by their Lord when they departed into the desert place. We notice they went by ship since by going that way the people could not follow. The apostles were to be in seclusion. This is something we need to keep in mind: when we have been busy in the Lord's work and it has been tiring, it may be the will of God that we take time out and rest. I am afraid some of us try to follow the Lord's guidance in every way, and yet we never hear Him say, "Come ye apart and rest."

I am reminded of something I saw years ago when I was a young Christian, teaching in a country community and boarding in a farm home there. After supper the mother prepared the little children for bed; after which she would come to the living room and sit alone, sometimes with a Bible in her lap, for perhaps half an hour. I have often thought since what a smart woman she was, taking time to rest, to let the day grow calm after all she had been through in the day. Caring for the children was strenuous, and she was involved with them constantly. She did not always read her Bible; but she would always wait in the presence of the Lord for that brief interval each evening. I remember how in my heart I thought, What a demonstration of "Come ye apart and rest awhile!"

Chapter 30

FEEDING THE FIVE THOUSAND

(Mark 6:33-44)

We are often inclined to think that if anything is being done as unto the Lord there is no need to pay attention to whether it is orderly or not, that God will bless it anyway. Such an impression can be misleading. I grew up in the country and I feel sure farmers would not be easily misled about this. They know very well that even if a farmer were a godly man, inclined to be devotional in his habits, he would still need to plant his seed at the right time in the right way. We saw it happen over and over that someone who was a fine man personally, was a poor farmer; and someone else who was really not a nice man personally, could be a good farmer. Being a poor or a good farmer would depend on how he carried on his activity according to the natural situation.

When the multitude followed Jesus of Nazareth into the open country to listen He took the occasion to demonstrate the power of God in an incident that Mark reports in chapter 6 (bracketed commentary is the author's):

> And the people saw them departing, [that is when Jesus of Nazareth and His disciples went by ship to the other side of the lake] and many knew him, and ran afoot thither out of all cities, and outwent them, and came together unto him. [He and His disciples crossed over in a ship but the crowd went around the outside of the lake and by hurrying they arrived by the time He did.] And Jesus, when he came out [I presume that means out of the boat] saw much people, and was moved with compassion toward them, because they were as sheep not having a shepherd: [this touched His heart] and he began to teach them many things (Mark 6:33-34).

What would be the condition of a sheep without a shepherd? Would it not mean that the sheep would be bewildered and uncertain, and perhaps frightened? And when He looked out upon these people and realized there was no one to lead them, He was deeply moved with compassion.

"And he began to teach them many things." What was He teaching them? Consider the Sermon on the Mount, and the parables He taught them. He kept showing them the ways of God, and this included the miracles He performed, demonstrating the power of God. He taught them both by explanation and by demonstration, showing them what God could do. We can be sure He talked for hours as He shared with them what they needed to know.

> And when the day was now far spent, his disciples came unto him, and said, This is a desert place, and now the time is far passed: send them away, that they may go into the country round about, and into the villages, and buy themselves bread: for they have nothing to eat (Mark 6:35-36).

The day was now far gone, because they had spent the day listening to Him. As nighttime came on they realized there was no food. "He answered and said unto them, Give ye them to eat" (Mark 6:37). I often wonder what they must have thought when He said that. Would there not be a very strong inclination to think that this was the most impractical person they had ever known? I sometimes think when we preach the gospel according to the way in which it actually reads, people will wonder about our good judgment.

> And they say unto him, Shall we go and buy two hundred penny-worth of bread, and give them to eat? He saith unto them, How many loaves have ye? go and see. And when they knew, they say, Five, and two fishes. And he commanded them to make all sit down by companies upon the green grass. And they sat down in ranks, by hundreds, and by fifties (Mark 6:37-40).

Let us pause here for a moment, as this is a vital point. After He had asked them what they had, and they had told Him, then He started to work. First, the disciples were told to go through the crowd and make them sit down in organized fashion. They sat in ranks by hundreds and by fifties. This was in order that they could be served; He did not want things to be helter-skelter. We know what He was planning to do: He was going to feed them. He was going to take the bread and fish and multiply that food in such a way that everyone would get something to eat.

> And when he had taken the five loaves and the two fishes, he looked up to heaven, and blessed, and brake the loaves, and gave them to his disciples to set before them; and the two fishes divided he among them all. And they did all eat, and were filled. And they took up twelve baskets full of the fragments, and of the fishes (Mark 6:41-43).

Many people reading the account of this event in the Bible are tempted to try to explain it, and they will offer first one idea and then another. Some will say those people just thought they were getting food, or they felt satisfied because their hunger was gone. But nothing in the world can explain away those twelve baskets of fragments. They had only five little loaves and two fishes and how in the world did they get twelve baskets of fragments? The inescapable fact is that the food was multiplied, and if you cannot see how that could be, neither can I. No one knows how it could be. But we do know one thing: with God nothing is impossible. Jesus of Nazareth knew this would be the way. "And they that did eat of the loaves were about five thousand men" (Mark 6:44). Only with God could that have been possible.

Let us look at this situation again: why were they made to sit down in companies of hundreds and fifties? Obviously it was easier to serve them from a practical point of view. Here is an amazing thing: the Lord was about to perform a miracle; but He wanted to go about it in an orderly fashion. It was not as if everyone opened his mouth and some fragments fell in. That is not how it happened. It was not done in any way that would be different from an ordinary procedure. These people were served bread and fish to eat, it was given to them in their hands, and they ate what they could, after which the fragments were taken up. Another item of interest is this: they did not leave the fragments lying around. Furthermore let us note that the fragments did not evaporate. Nothing in this whole event was so extraordinary in any other way, except one thing: the food was multiplied; and that is what it was all about.

In the matter of the preaching and the teaching of the gospel the actual instruction should be practical, the actual talking will be human. A man should speak clearly and forcefully, and he should talk to people in a natural and effectual fashion. That is not where the miracle comes in. The miracle comes when the people believe in God from what they have heard; and God then does something else. God blesses the Word so that it will not return unto Him void, but it will accomplish that to which He sent it.

Chapter 31

OPEN DISPLAY OF POWER

(Mark 6:45-56)

As Jesus of Nazareth went about to manifest the reality of God among men He followed at least two lines of approach. In the first place He told about the ways of God, often using parables and appealing to their reason and logic, to show them how consistently and how rationally the ways of God in the spiritual world followed the very ways of God in the natural world. First the seed, then the ear, then the full corn in the ear. The second thing He did was to show the mighty power of God in doing works of wonder. He showed the mighty power of God in performing miracles. In various miracles He demonstrated the power of God over the processes of nature. He showed how God can control what goes on in the natural world. Such works were not so much anti-natural as they were super-natural. If a man was blind He did not make that man see with his ears; that would be contrary to nature. He made him see with his eyes (that's what they were for), which meant He healed the man's eyes.

When first studying these miracles I said to myself: this is not magic. This is not something contrary to nature. It is an unusual way in which someone can make the natural processes work more directly. Jesus made a man see with his eyes and hear with his ears by restoring the eyes and ears to their function, and this represents part of what the Lord Jesus came to do. He came to man who was diseased in sin and sick with his own iniquities, and He caused that man to be well, the way God at first intended him to be. Sometimes He performed a certain miracle several times, as if to emphasize. And that is the way we will develop the portion we have today. A similar incident occurred before in this record of Mark but now we will turn to Mark 6:45. He had just finished feeding the five thousand.

> And straightway he constrained his disciples to get into the ship, and to go to the other side before unto Bethsaida, while he sent away the people (Mark 6:45).

All this seems deceptively simple. But what is happening? To accomplish His purpose He managed practical arrangements. He planned to take those men to the other side of the lake. His was not some magical action to sweep them up in a cloud and deposit them over there. He did not snap His fingers and have them suddenly moved from one side of the lake to the other. They went in a boat. He told them to get in the boat while He sent the people away; He did not just wave a wand to accomplish that. Although He had just displayed the power of God in a marvelous way in feeding five thousand people with a few loaves and fishes, He turned right around and made practical arrangements to reduce practical everyday pressure in a normal way.

"And when he had sent them away, he departed into a mountain to pray" (Mark 6:46). Under the pressure of events, having just fed five thousand people, He takes time out to go to the top of the mountain to pray. Prayer is far more important than we ordinarily think it is. When you and I may wonder whether or not we should take time to pray, we should remember how He did. Many would be ready offhand to think, "If I should sin I should pray." This is true, and it is wonderful to turn to God when we sin. But when I am in doubt or in fear or in some kind of trouble I should pray. Jesus of Nazareth had not sinned but He went to pray. He had no doubt about what He was going to do, but He went to pray to the Father. There is far more in prayer than just asking help when I am weak. There is more in prayer than just asking for forgiveness when I am wrong, or direction when I am confused. There is something about prayer that made this One, a perfect person, take time out to turn to His Father in prayer.

The praise, the worship, the communion in which He fellowshiped with the Father, no doubt strengthened Him physically. Undoubtedly He received grace in these experiences; but it is worthy of note that as strong as He was, as able as He was (He had just fed five thousand people), and as remarkably capable as He showed Himself to be in doing amazing things (He was about to walk on the water); He took time out to go off into the mountains to pray.

"And when even was come, the ship was in the midst of the sea, and he alone on the land" (Mark 6:47). The disciples were doing as He had directed them. He had departed into a mountain to pray. They were in the midst of the sea, because He was sending them across, but He was not with them in person.

And he saw them toiling in rowing; for the wind was contrary unto them: and about the fourth watch of the night he cometh unto them, walking upon the sea, and would have passed by them (Mark 6:48).

"He saw them toiling in rowing." He had told them to go without Him, but He kept His eye on them. He knew what was happening. You and I can read this with much interest. We can be sure that when we are in trouble, when we are toiling in rowing, striving to make our way in what we are doing, He is watching over us.

Anyone who has ever rowed a boat will get the picture. I remember not long ago being in a small boat on a lake. A strong wind was blowing and I was coming in from fishing because it had become too windy. I was making about four or five miles an hour and rowing into a wind that was blowing ten miles an hour. I amused myself for some time trying to figure out how long it would take me to get across that lake, if I rowed five miles an hour and the wind was blowing ten miles an hour against me. This experience of the disciples was much more serious. Those men were in a storm; a literal translation of the Greek brings out this phrase, "they digged furiously." Here Mark simply records they were digging, toiling in rowing. "For the wind was contrary unto them."

We should remember why they were there. He had sent them. He had personally told them "Go across that lake." This is what they were doing, and the wind was contrary to them. Can we learn from this? Even though I am doing exactly what I should do, I may have trouble. But it is a comfort to note that even though He was not personally present with them, He watched over them. This reminds us of the promise: "I will never leave thee, nor forsake thee." He had directed them into the boat for that very journey, and now the circumstances were not favorable. I may be doing exactly the thing I am supposed to be doing, and trouble can be right at my doorstep blowing in on me. I may be in the will of God and find my circumstances contrary, but I should wait, the story isn't finished. "And about the fourth watch of the night he cometh unto them, walking upon the sea, and would have passed by them" (Mark 6:48).

They were struggling to get across the lake. The wind kept blowing against them; and then when they saw Him, to their dismay, He seemed about to pass by!

But when they saw him walking upon the sea, they supposed it had been a spirit, and cried out: for they all saw him, and were troubled. And immediately he talked with them, and saith unto them, Be of good cheer: it is I; be not afraid. And he went up unto them into the ship; and the wind

> ceased: and they were sore amazed in themselves beyond measure, and wondered (Mark 6:49-51).

Has God done wonders for us, and yet we fear what will happen tomorrow? Is it possible we have been blessed and blessed, yet tremble when we think about the days to come? That is how it was with them. And this could be true of me because my heart is hardened. Otherwise I would take what I understand, and I would know that the God who blessed me yesterday is the same God who is watching over me today and will be with me tomorrow.

It is not surprising to read the account of the effect this miracle had upon the people in that region. They were ready to believe Jesus of Nazareth could do anything He wanted to do. They were impressed to think He would be gracious and so they brought the sick to Him that they might be healed (Mark 6:53-56).

Chapter 32

ANSWERING CRITICS

(Mark 7:1-23)

One of the big handicaps that the gospel must endure is that it is handled by men. The simple and awful fact is that when men are involved in any operation it will be faulty. We have heard people say there is nothing wrong with the world: it is the people in it. That is true and we could say it with reference to churches!

Children are not born with any knowledge of God. They may have an inward disposition to honor Him and they may be inclined in a certain way to obey, but they do not know. They must learn about Him, and they must learn this from other human beings. This is where the rub comes in, because other human beings are not perfect; yet they have to deal with this great truth. No wonder Paul says we have this treasure in earthen vessels (2 Cor. 4:7). In helping children and others to learn, people act as teachers and as leaders. When people get together to do something they choose someone to be their leader. It is characteristic of these men when they lead to develop their own style and their own procedures. This is commonly seen in church practices. The common tendency in the church is to withdraw from anyone who is not like us, and then we avoid those who are not of our group. Some will say, for instance, if one hasn't been baptized in a certain way he doesn't even belong, although that way is not clearly pointed out in Scripture. All kinds of various doctrines and teachings are based upon human ideas of these things.

> Then came together unto him the Pharisees, and certain of the scribes, which came from Jerusalem. And when they saw some of his disciples eat bread with defiled, that is to say, with unwashen, hands, they found fault (Mark 7:1-2).

That does not mean their hands were dirty. This is not a matter of hygiene, this is a matter of procedure, of custom. There was a certain way in which they were supposed to act.

> For the Pharisees, and all the Jews, except they wash their hands oft, eat not, holding the tradition of the elders. And when they come from the market, except they wash, they eat not. And many other things there be, which they have received to hold, as the washing of cups, and pots, brazen vessels, and of tables. Then the Pharisees and scribes asked him, Why walk not thy disciples according to the tradition of the elders, but eat bread with unwashen hands? (Mark 7:3-5).

It is important to remember this was not referring to washing plates to get them clean, or washing hands for practical reasons. This is referring to the ceremony; doing this thing officially as it were. For instance, when we go to the Lord's Supper and eat the bread and drink the cup, we do not go there to get a meal. Some churches are trying to reproduce the details of that event, but generally speaking the little bit of bread and the little sip of the cup taken in the course of the Lord's Supper is not really a supper, but it does represent something vitally important. That bread represents the body of Jesus Christ, and that cup represents everything that was in the cross of Calvary, and we partake of it in that fashion. Men are inclined to add other things. In those days among the Jews and Pharisees, this is what had happened. They had a way of making it a point of washing their hands to make themselves "clean," acceptable; the disciples of Jesus of Nazareth did not do that. From such a background the question was raised: "Why walk not thy disciples according to the tradition of the elders?" Their conduct would not be according to the Scriptures, but according to the tradition of the elders. But Jesus of Nazareth dealt sharply with these critics:

> He answered and said unto them, Well hath Isaiah prophesied of you hypocrites, as it is written, This people honoreth me with their lips, but their heart is far from me (Mark 7:6).

The meaning of this Scripture seems quite clear. "They talk as if they were worshiping me, but they are not."

Take the matter of going to church: this is extremely important and I am in favor of it, but do you realize that people can go to church and not worship God? There are people who make a point of this: they feel when they go to church they have done what they should have done, although they may not listen to the preacher, or take any part in the service. Jesus of Nazareth pointed out that it is what is in the heart that counts. He continued His discussion by quoting Isaiah:

> He answered and said unto them, Well hath Isaiah prophesied of you hypocrites, as it is written, This people honoreth me with their lips, but their heart is far from me. Howbeit

> in vain do they worship me, teaching for doctrines the commandments of men. For laying aside the commandment of God, ye hold the tradition of men, as the washing of pots and cups: and many other such like things ye do. And he said unto them, Full well ye reject the commandment of God, that ye may keep your own tradition. For Moses said, Honor thy father and thy mother; and, Whoso curseth father or mother, let him die the death: but ye say, If a man shall say to his father or mother, It is Corban, that is to say, a gift, by whatsoever thou mightest be profited by me; he shall be free (Mark 7:6-11).

Perhaps that is not too clear so let me be just a little more specific: the Israelites had a custom that if a man offered anything to the priest the regulation that he should give it to his parents would no longer apply. He had offered it to the priest. If a man had earned wages, instead of bringing the wages to his parents as the law of Moses required, he would bring them to the priest, and give him a token – a little bit. Bringing his wages and offering them to the priest would satisfy his obligation; he could keep the rest of it. The Lord was saying the whole purpose of the Scriptures was defeated at this point.

> And ye suffer him no more to do aught for his father or his mother; making the word of God of none effect through your tradition, which ye have delivered: and many such like things do ye (Mark 7:12-13).

I will purposely avoid making any application of this principle in actual church life, because some congregations do things differently and it might seem I am talking against certain groups. Even among the most spiritually minded there are people like that: unless a person has had the experiences they have had, that person does not count. This is not what the Bible teaches, but this is how some act.

> And when he had called all the people unto him, he said unto them, Hearken unto me every one of you, and understand: there is nothing from without a man, that entering into him can defile him: but the things which come out of him, those are they that defile the man (Mark 7:14-15).

This astonishing statement says simply it is not what comes from the outside of a man that counts: it is what comes from the inside of a man that counts. It is not what a man looks like, but it is what he is thinking. "For as he thinketh in his heart, so is he" (Prov. 23:7). It is not what I do or how I do, but it is what I was thinking when I did it. Why do I read my Bible? Just to be reading? or do I read the Bible to learn the Word of God? Why do I pray? Just because I want to say I prayed or because I want the blessing of God? Why do I place an offering on the offering plate? Do I place it there because it is a regulation? Or do I do it because I want to share in the work of the Lord? The difference in these attitudes is noted by the Lord.

By the way: how much difference does it make to you if you see the preacher is wearing a gown or not wearing a gown? Do you think the clerical gown will make any difference in the sermon? Do you think the frequent use of certain words (i.e. some people say "Amen," and other people say "Hallelujah" or "Praise the Lord") adds anything? It is doubtless true that some people could mean those things, but do not some people say such things just out of habit? Does all of this mean that any style is as good as another? Actually it means that any style is good when we mean it from the heart as we practice it.

God sees the heart and if we mean to serve Him we can do it any way we want to. There is no rule. And if we do not mean to serve Him, again there is no rule; nothing is good enough unless we mean it from the heart. This is the way the Lord answered the criticism based upon breaking tradition and not following custom.

Chapter 33

MORE WORKS OF WONDER

(Mark 7:24–8:9)

The New Testament in its records shows much of the methods used by Jesus of Nazareth to tell the truth about God, to communicate the gospel. If we study those and see how it went with Jesus of Nazareth as He was teaching and preaching, we will notice He taught not by using explanation but by descriptions. He did not explain but He told how it happened. The ways of God are past finding out. The Holy Spirit guided in preparing the gospel and that would mean that what we have recorded is chosen material given to us for the purposes the Holy Spirit had in mind. John tells us in the course of his Gospel:

> And many other signs truly did Jesus in the presence of his disciples, which are not written in this book: but these are written, that ye might believe that Jesus is the Christ, the Son of God; and that believing ye might have life through his name (John 20:30-31).

Later he said again:

> And there are also many other things which Jesus did, the which, if they should be written every one, I suppose that even the world itself could not contain the books that should be written (John 21:25).

We gather that John knew very well he was not telling everything. He did not tell of all the times the Lord Jesus exercised the power of God, but certain ones were chosen on purpose, and these he has described.

We can believe that Mark did it in the same way, and so when we read his record we learn there are repeated accounts of certain types of work. For instance, the walking on the waters: there are at least two accounts of that. The opening of the eyes of the blind and making the lame to walk are other instances. This is done to give the reader a true impression of Jesus of Nazareth. The works Jesus of Nazareth did were not exceptional in the sense of once and for all; this is the kind of thing He did over and over again while He was here. When we think about Jesus of Nazareth being known far and wide we are not to think it is because some one thing happened; we are to remember that is because over and over again this is the way He did. People began to have a great interest in and a great esteem for Jesus of Nazareth.

We come now to one of these incidents:

> And from thence he arose, and went into the borders of Tyre and Sidon, and entered into a house, and would have no man know it: but he could not be hid. For a certain woman, whose young daughter had an unclean spirit, heard of him, and came and fell at his feet (Mark 7:24-25).

To say that the daughter had an unclean spirit does not mean she was immoral; it does not mean there was anything improper about her conduct; it means unclean in the sense that it was not according to the will of God. This was a spirit not subject to God, we might call it "an evil spirit." It could have been said to be "an angel of the devil." These words would all have various connotations, but they would all be included in the saying it was "an unclean spirit." This certain woman whose daughter had an unclean spirit heard of Him and came and fell at His feet.

> The woman was a Greek, a Syrophenician by nation; and she besought him that he would cast forth the devil out of her daughter (Mark 7:26).

According to the New Testament, salvation is of the Jews; that is to say, it originates there. But salvation is not limited to Jews; it is for everyone, as this incident showed.

> But Jesus said unto her, Let the children first be filled: for it is not meet to take the children's bread, and to cast it unto the dogs (Mark 7:27).

This was a statement He made by way of testing the woman's attitude and faith. The word "filled" means "satisfied" and the children referred to those who were the children of God. Let the people who belong to God first be satisfied. And He says it is not meet, it is not fitting, to take the children's bread and cast it unto "the dogs." You will remember that among the people in those days it was customary for the Jewish people in their idiom to speak of Gentiles as "dogs," and so He made this comment.

> And she answered and said unto him, Yes, Lord: yet the dogs under the table eat of the children's crumbs. And he said unto her, For this saying go thy way; the devil is gone out of thy daughter (Mark 7:28-29).

He is saying to her in effect: "It is wonderful that you understand this." In one of the other Gospels it is expressed this way:

"Great is thy faith." In what sense was her faith great? Her faith was not only in Jesus of Nazareth to heal her daughter, but her faith also included that He, as a son of David and in line with Old Testament prophecy, would heal her daughter even though she was a Gentile. The passage: "In him shall the Gentiles trust" is in the Old Testament; and so this woman came in this way and this is what He recognized. She knew the Jews had a view that would leave her out, but she also knew that God had a view that brought her in, and she came on the strength of that. So she answered Him in the language He used: "Yet the dogs under the table eat of the children's crumbs" and that, in effect, was what she was asking for. She showed that she understood He came for everyone.

"And when she was come to her house, she found the devil gone out, and her daughter laid upon the bed" (Mark 7:30). She had been delivered, and from that we can draw a profound truth for ourselves: understanding the plan of salvation helps faith in prayer. She was confident in praying, because she understood the gospel well enough to know it was not limited to one class of people; it was for everyone.

We read what followed:

> And again, departing from the coasts of Tyre and Sidon, he came unto the Sea of Galilee, through the midst of the coasts of Decapolis. And they bring unto him one that was deaf, and had an impediment in his speech; and they beseech him to put his hand upon him. And he took him aside from the multitude, and put his fingers into his ears, and he spit, and touched his tongue; and looking up to heaven, he sighed, and saith unto him, Ephphatha, that is, Be opened. And straightway his ears were opened, and the string of his tongue was loosed, and he spake plain. And he charged them that they should tell no man: but the more he charged them, so much the more a great deal they published it; and were beyond measure astonished, saying, He hath done all things well: he maketh both the deaf to hear, and the dumb to speak (Mark 7:31-37).

This incident comes to us with great emphasis to show He was able to heal because He had the power.

> In those days the multitude being very great, and having nothing to eat, Jesus called his disciples unto him, and saith unto them, I have compassion on the multitude, because they have now been with me three days, and have nothing to eat: and if I send them away fasting to their own houses, they will faint by the way: for divers of them came from far. And his disciples answered him, From whence can a man satisfy these men with bread here in the wilderness? And he asked them, How many loaves have ye? And they said, Seven. And he commanded the people to sit down on

> the ground: and he took the seven loaves, and gave thanks, and brake, and gave to his disciples to set before them; and they did set them before the people. And they had a few small fishes: and he blessed, and commanded to set them also before them. So they did eat, and were filled: and they took up of the broken meat that was left seven baskets. And they that had eaten were about four thousand: and he sent them away (Mark 8:1-9).

Let me emphasize this. "I have compassion on the multitude." Don't you think there would be some unbelievers in the multitude? I think there would be. And this brings to my mind something like this: a person living in a community where there are believers will oftentimes be blessed even though he himself has no faith. I do not mean he will be saved, but he will be benefited, because he is living where these other people live. And so, as we meditate here upon all these things, we say "He is the Lord. He doeth all things well."

Chapter 34

PRIORITY OF FAITH

(Mark 8:10-26)

If you hear a message claiming to be the true gospel how can you test it for genuineness? I am sure you will agree right away: one cannot tell by the way a man talks. Some men may talk smoothly and yet not be telling the truth, and some men may talk disconnectedly, never getting anything said right because of excitement. Yet they might know the truth. We cannot recognize the truth by the way a message is expressed. While He was here Jesus of Nazareth sought to win believers to God through the gospel He preached. Everything He said and did was to the end that men should believe. The gospel deals with invisible realities, so if we just say those words, what will it mean to the man who has never seen what we are talking about? How can one ever be sure that such a preacher who is setting forth the gospel is telling the truth?

The Old Testament Scriptures warned the people of God against impostors; and the peril of deception among the people of God is an ever present threat. It can happen any time. Jesus of Nazareth warned: "Be not deceived." And this master of deception: the enemy, the devil, has all kinds of ideas to deceive us. They sound like the gospel but they are not true. Earnest people have been cautioned in the Bible to beware lest they be deceived. "Let no man deceive you by any means" is what the Bible tells us.

Mark records how a person can be sure:

> And straightway he entered into a ship with his disciples, and came into the parts of Dalmanutha. And the Pharisees came forth, and began to question with him, seeking of him a sign from heaven, tempting him. And he sighed deeply in his spirit, and saith, Why doth this generation seek after a sign? verily I say unto you, There shall no sign be given unto this generation (Mark 8:10-12).

If we should ask why they were looking for a sign, we should remember it was because that is what the Old Testament told them to do. If a prophet came and professed to be a man from God, bringing a message from God, the people were instructed to ask him for some evidence, some sign only God could provide. This was what they did. They wanted Jesus of Nazareth to show them the label under which He was operating.

History records there were signs enough because the signs would be in the fruit. At this point the other Gospels report that He said there would be no sign given to this generation except the sign of the prophet Jonah. In Matthew He plainly states as Jonah was three days in the belly of the whale, so shall the Son of Man be three days in the bowels of the earth. The resurrection of Jesus Christ would be the only sign that would be given. But here Mark is leaving it strictly the way it reads, and this was exclusive for believers who would understand.

After this Jesus of Nazareth emphasized the priority of faith.

> And he left them, and entering into the ship again departed to the other side. Now the disciples had forgotten to take bread, neither had they in the ship with them more than one loaf. And he charged them, saying, Take heed, beware of the leaven of the Pharisees, and of the leaven of Herod. And they reasoned among themselves, saying, It is because we have no bread. And when Jesus knew it, he saith unto them, Why reason ye, because ye have no bread? perceive ye not yet, neither understand? have ye your heart yet hardened? Having eyes, see ye not? and having ears, hear ye not? and do ye not remember? When I brake the five loaves among five thousand, how many baskets full of fragments took ye up? They say unto him, Twelve. And when the seven among four thousand, how many baskets full of fragments took ye up? And they said, Seven. And he said unto them, How is it that ye do not understand? (Mark 8:13-21).

As a matter of fact, all this had been demonstrated before them in certain consequences when Jesus of Nazareth took action; results followed and they were sufficient evidence. He took the opportunity of the natural request of the people to teach them. People learn more quickly and more fully when their questions are answered. He taught them to beware of the leaven of the Pharisees, and of the leaven of Herod (referred to in the other Gospels as the leaven of the Sadducees). The word "leaven" refers to the bread, and He is using it as a figure of speech here.

The "leaven of the Pharisees" refers to the doctrine they taught and if one would receive their doctrine it was like eating their bread: their ideas would be absorbed. The Pharisees were influenced by outward fulfillment. According to them, if one wanted to know whether anything was truly of God, he would want to know if it had been done in the right way, on the right day, by someone dressed the right way. This is a snare.

The "leaven of Herod" would be the ideas of those people who were teaching and preaching a certain political aspect of human conduct. The Sadducees would be emphasizing a rational way of living. This would be rather hard to understand, I suspect, for many of us. The Pharisees said you will know if you are right with God if you do things at the right time in the right way; the Sadducees would say you would know you are right with God if you understand, if you can explain what you are doing. It is a great temptation to feel that if I do anything the right way (in the church, when I am dressed in a certain way, under certain circumstances), then I am pretty good. The Sadducees would say they were only going to believe the things they could understand. We read elsewhere in the Bible they denied the resurrection; the reality of heaven; the existence of angels; the existence of a spirit; and the reality of Satan.

Such ideas can get into the mind. A person could get the idea that his way of living and doing should be acceptable to God because he keeps all the rules. Another person could feel satisfied with the way he thinks because he understands it. The one would be a Pharisee, the other a Sadducee; and both would be wrong. The truth is that anything is true if God is working in it. It must be said about the Pharisees they believed the Scriptures were the Word of God, but they had added things to the Scriptures which were wrong; herein was the snare. They still believed in the Bible; but that could not be said of the Sadduces. They did not believe the Scriptures. As I read the New Testament I do not find that one Sadducee is on record as ever being saved, although some Pharisees were saved.

At the end of this chapter we come to a case in point:

> And he cometh to Bethsaida; and they bring a blind man unto him, and besought him to touch him. And he took the blind man by the hand, and led him out of the town; and when he had spit on his eyes, and put his hands upon him, he asked him if he saw aught. And he looked up, and said, I see men as trees, walking. After that he put his hands again upon his eyes, and made him look up: and he was restored, and saw every man clearly. And he sent him away to his house, saying, Neither go into the town, nor tell it to any in the town (Mark 8:22-26).

This is not the way the Pharisees would have done it. They would have done it in the "right" way. And this is not the way the Sadducees would have done it. They would have acted in a way you could understand. But Jesus of Nazareth did it the way God would do it. The difference was in the procedure. The fruit of the gospel that really shows is the power of God and His working in changed lives. Blind men come to see and then we know we have the truth.

Chapter 35

PETER'S CONFESSION

(Mark 8:27-38)

There can be no doubt in anyone's mind that the name of Jesus Christ is related to great things in this world. He cannot be dismissed whether one trusts in Him or not. He cannot be counted as insignificant. But it does make a great deal of difference what you think of Him, and what I think of Him.

When the Lord Jesus was speaking to His disciples He said, "Whom do men say that I am?" It is interesting to notice the replies. Some said: "John the Baptist," who was probably the greatest preacher they knew anything about. Some said: "Elias," who was one of the greatest prophets in their history. Some said merely: "One of the prophets" (Mark 8:27-28). Each of these names refers to some great person, but not one of them is true. It is not enough to say that Jesus Christ was great. All of the wonderful things done in His name may all be very good, but even this is not really adequate.

Jesus of Nazareth pressed another question: "Whom say ye that I am?" Peter spoke for the group when he said: "Thou art the Christ." This was important but Christ Jesus did not want this identification to be made in public at that time. He commanded them not to tell anyone.

> And he began to teach them, that the Son of man must suffer many things, and be rejected of the elders, and of the chief priests, and scribes, and be killed, and after three days rise again (Mark 8:31).

This was told to the disciples. As they listened they were shocked. When you and I think of these things it is hard for us to put ourselves in the place of those people. The One they were following, the One they were listening to, the One they were watching, the One whom they had seen perform miracles: this One must suffer these things!

Some of us may think when we suffer it must be because we are bad, or because we have done something wrong. The Lord Jesus was not bad, and He had not done anything wrong, yet

He had to suffer many things. Suffering is not directly related to conduct: suffering may well originate in something else or someone else who has in mind to do us harm. Here we should remember how the Son of Man said He must suffer many things and be rejected. In fact He said: "Be rejected of the elders." It would be the leading people who would reject this Person. He would be rejected by the chief priests in the temple among the very people who were worshiping God. The Son of Man was to be rejected and finally killed, and then He would rise again the third day.

Peter began to rebuke Him. We need not think this was presumptuous on Peter's part. We do not know all that Peter had in mind. I have always felt that Peter had in mind to say: "You do not need to do this; you do not deserve this kind of treatment. Considering all you have done for them, this is not fair and you deserve better treatment." No doubt Peter meant well but he was wrong; because those who walk in the ways of God will have trouble and should be ready to expect it and to endure it.

> But when he had turned about and looked on his disciples, he rebuked Peter, saying, Get thee behind me, Satan: for thou savorest not the things that be of God, but the things that be of men (Mark 8:33).

This word "savor" is not commonly used among us unless we speak of savory meat; but it has to do with taste. This is a way of saying, "You do not taste like the things of God; you taste like the things of men." What would taste like men? Peter's words suggest that He avoid trouble so that He could be at ease. Peter suggested He not do the will of God but rather what would sound good to man. This was the line of thought Jesus of Nazareth rebuked.

> And when he had called the people unto him with his disciples also, he said unto them, Whosoever will come after me, let him deny himself, and take up his cross, and follow me (Mark 8:34).

It is a common tendency for any of us to think of any particular trouble we have, such as rheumatism or a weak stomach, as a cross. It may be parents will have an unruly child, and they may call that their "cross." I do not mean to say such things are not real and serious, but not one is a cross in this sense. "Taking up your cross" would be following Jesus Christ to Calvary and yielding yourself to Him. He then makes this general statement:

> For whosoever will save his life shall lose it; but whosoever shall lose his life for my sake and the gospel's, the same shall save it (Mark 8:35).

Let us note carefully the way this is expressed. This does not mean that "whosoever loses his life" by just wasting himself is going to save it. Notice again what He said and then added:

> For what shall it profit a man, if he shall gain the whole world, and lose his own soul? Or what shall a man give in exchange for his soul? (Mark 8:36-37).

Here the Lord Jesus put His finger on a (tremendously important) basic truth.

The Lord Jesus through the Holy Spirit may confront me any day when I am going about doing things and ask me point blank:

> For what shall it profit a man, if he shall gain the whole world, and lose his own soul? Or what shall a man give in exchange for his soul? Whosoever therefore shall be ashamed of me and of my words in this adulterous and sinful generation; of him also shall the Son of man be ashamed, when he cometh in the glory of his Father with the holy angels (Mark 8:36-38).

You and I are to have this in mind: the way we live and the way we follow the Lord Jesus Christ is so important that if we shrink from it, if we fail to follow Him or yield to Him, we are sure to suffer the consequences.

In these words Jesus of Nazareth put forth an extremely important truth. As I live my life I am constantly being challenged in various ways and in these challenges there is always an angle that refers me to the Lord Jesus Christ. It may be that I am challenged to give, to share, and I feel in my heart this is what the Lord wants of me; but if I do not do that, it is not just a matter of being ashamed that I belong in that company, it is actually a matter of my being ashamed of His program. "Of him also shall the Son of man be ashamed, when he cometh in the glory of his Father with the holy angels."

At this point we should underscore something: Jesus Christ is coming back and He is coming in the glory of His Father. He is coming with His holy angels and at that time those who stood with Him in testimony now will be with Him in glory then. It is tremendously important that we remember this.

Chapter 36

THE TRANSFIGURATION

(Mark 9:1-13)

Jesus of Nazareth had called His disciples, some of whom He made His apostles, to be with Him that He might teach them. He wanted to teach them what He had to show to the whole world. What He wanted to reveal was oftentimes beyond words, which would not be adequate, so He demonstrated by actions on His part. We will note now how He taught them about the actual facts of the kingdom of God. We have heard the phrase "the kingdom of God" many times. I do not know what the kingdom of God would appear to be in the average person's mind, but when we think of kingdoms we usually think of geographical areas, cities: and then we think of commerce, trade, and of all the things that go together to make a country great. We would speak about such things being the kingdom, especially in the days when there were kings: all that was in the king's dominion. If he had ships, there would be many ships; if he had soldiers, there would be many soldiers, etc.

Now when this term is used with reference to the things of God, as when we speak of the kingdom of God, we must revise our thinking. The kingdom of God is different from what we think. Often we conceive of it in external magnificence, so that when people talk about heaven it may seem as if we were thinking about some vast pyrotechnical display: like the fair-grounds on the last night of the fair, when fireworks illumine the sky. Some think the kingdom of God would be greater than that, as if it were a massive celebration type of thing from a human point of view. But such thinking is wrong: that is not the way. I am satisfied heaven will be glorious and there will be great and wonderful things there, but such earthly magnificence is not the essence of the kingdom of God.

The kingdom of God is in us and Jesus of Nazareth now showed this to His disciples.

> And he said unto them, Verily I say unto you, That there be some of them that stand here, which shall not taste of

> death, till they have seen the kingdom of God come with power. And after six days Jesus taketh with him Peter, and James, and John, and leadeth them up into a high mountain apart by themselves: and he was transfigured before them. And his raiment became shining, exceeding white as snow; so as no fuller on earth can white them. And there appeared unto them Elijah with Moses: and they were talking with Jesus (Mark 9:1-4).

I wonder if we can by any means understand how those apostles must have felt? Can we have any idea what an amazing thing this was to them? Here was this Person with whom they had traveled day in and day out, transfigured before them. Even His clothing was changed. Nothing was put on Him from the outside. This was not something dropped over Him, like a shroud or cape put over His shoulders, or anything like that. This was from the inside out. Was it something in His physical body of such a nature it could suddenly cause His whole body to be transfigured? In another place we read His face was as bright as the shining of the sun. What about His clothing? His raiment became glistening white; that wasn't from the outside. This was some hidden element that suddenly now became visible. It revealed Him; it was something done by which He was being revealed. The clothing He had was revealed as other clothing that was glistening white. We do not know what color of clothing He had on but it was not glistening white. This clothing He now had was so white no one on earth had ever laundered anything to look like it.

I want us to grasp if we can, what Peter, James and John saw. Much was left unsaid, I know; but there is much said. We may note in passing that in the spiritual realm there is no death. Elijah was there with Moses to commune with Jesus of Nazareth. It was all overwhelming to the three disciples.

> And Peter answered and said to Jesus, Master, it is good for us to be here: and let us make three tabernacles; one for thee, and one for Moses, and one for Elijah. For he wist not what to say; for they were sore afraid (Mark 9:5-6).

This is tremendous! As we think about Peter there are many times we may feel he was impulsive, and we know that on occasions he made mistakes; but before we are through thinking about Peter we should remember Peter was taken up on the Mount of Transfiguration. He saw the transfigured Lord there and talked to Him.

Why a tabernacle for each? The tabernacle in the Old Testament was a place to worship. Were these to be like shrines? Did he have in mind that they could come to worship these persons? Why would they worship Moses and Elijah? Or were these shrines just to be built to commune with them or to confer with them? The sight of Moses would bring to mind that he was one who was known for saying, "This is the word of God, do it." Elijah was the great prophet who stressed when you worship God you should mean it. And Jesus of Nazareth who would say, "Obey. Even if it kills you, obey." These were the three who were talking together while Peter, James and John were watching.

> And there was a cloud that overshadowed them: and a voice came out of the cloud, saying, This is my beloved Son: hear him (Mark 9:7).

The other occasion when Mark reports a voice from heaven was at the time of the baptism of John the Baptist (Mark 1:11).

> And suddenly, when they had looked round about, they saw no man any more, save Jesus only with themselves (Mark 9:8).

This event happened as it was told. No one can explain it. There are things about it that are absolutely beyond our understanding. We need to notice this is the way Jesus of Nazareth taught His disciples what the kingdom of God was. It is the indwelling of God, coming in to us.

> And as they came down from the mountain, he charged them that they should tell no man what things they had seen, till the Son of man were risen from the dead (Mark 9:9).

I do not know what Jesus of Nazareth had in mind; I only wish I could be clear enough in my own mind that I could just do what He says. Jesus told them not to talk about this. If I were to give any suggestions it would come to my mind to say that no one would understand what they were talking about, anyway. So let us keep quiet until the resurrection takes place, then we shall see and then we shall know.

When this was finished they were questioning one another as to what this should mean: "And they kept that saying with themselves, questioning one with another what the rising from the dead should mean." He had told them He would rise from the dead. He had told them He would be rejected by the chief priests and all the others. But now they actually did not know what He meant when He said He would rise from the dead. While we are thinking of these things we can ask the Lord to help us grasp this great truth: the kingdom of God is within us, and all that is involved in the presence of God is the important part of the gospel. The Lord will be in us and with us doing His work, to will and to do in us of His good pleasure.

At this point in our study we should learn something about the interpretation of predictive prophecy. Jesus of Nazareth had told them He would be killed and rise from the dead on the third day (Mark 8:31). And now when He gave them instructions as to how they should do when He was "risen from the dead," they were "questioning one with another what the rising from the dead should mean." After the resurrection had actually occurred there was no confusion about what it meant. From this I form the opinion that prophecies that refer to His Second Coming may cause discussion and confusion among interpreters now because the event has not yet occurred.

> And they asked him, saying, Why say the scribes that Elijah must first come? And he answered and told them, Elijah verily cometh first, and restoreth all things; and how it is written of the Son of man, that he must suffer many things, and be set at nought. But I say unto you, That Elijah is indeed come, and they have done unto him whatsoever they listed, as it is written of him (Mark 9:11-13).

Mark does not offer any help in understanding this saying of Jesus of Nazareth, but Matthew points out that "He spake unto them of John the Baptist" (Matt. 17:13). Here we see again how believers could have the Scriptures in hand with all confidence in them as being the Word of God, and yet have no clear idea what the fulfillment would look like before the event actually occurred. In the same line of insight it can be understood that all predictions in the Word of God will be found to be exactly true when the predicted events occur. The written Scriptures will then help to show the events to be authentic because they were predicted in the foreknowledge of God, e.g. John 13:19 and John 16:4.

Chapter 37

THE HEALING OF THE AFFLICTED SON

(Mark 9:14-29)

Immediately after the transfiguration Jesus of Nazareth came upon a situation that has much to say to us.

> And when he came to his disciples, he saw a great multitude about them, and the scribes questioning with them. And straightway all the people, when they beheld him, were greatly amazed, and running to him saluted him. And he asked the scribes, What question ye with them? (Mark 9:14-16).

It was a matter of interest to Jesus of Nazareth and the three disciples as to what caused this crowd of people to be so greatly stirred about what had happened. They were discussing this among themselves when they saw Him, and they came quickly to get some answer to their questions. At once it was revealed what it was these people were so concerned about.

> And one of the multitude answered and said, Master, I have brought unto thee my son, which hath a dumb spirit; and wheresoever he taketh him, he teareth him: and he foameth, and gnasheth with his teeth, and pineth away: and I spake to thy disciples that they should cast him out; and they could not (Mark 9:17-18).

This was the simple, sad story of how a father brought his son to Jesus of Nazareth, and in the absence of the Lord he talked to the disciples, asking for deliverance. The disciples undertook to deliver the son but they could not. The fact that this happened caused great excitement. The people were noticing something different. Ordinarily when men or children who were sick or in trouble had been brought to Jesus of Nazareth or to His disciples they would be healed. So in this case when nothing happened it was astonishing and upsetting. Why did not something happen?

> He answereth him, and said, O faithless generation, how long shall I be with you? how long shall I suffer you? bring him unto me (Mark 9:19).

There seems to be implied here some tone of rebuke possibly to the disciples and maybe to the group as a whole, and He implies that this development was disappointing to Him. Then He gives this word:

> How long shall I suffer you? bring him unto me. And they brought him unto him: and when he saw him, straightway the spirit tare him; and he fell on the ground, and wallowed foaming. And he asked his father, How long is it ago since this came unto him? And he said, Of a child. And ofttimes it hath cast him into the fire, and into the waters, to destroy him: but if thou canst do any thing, have compassion on us, and help us (Mark 9:19-22).

So far as I have noticed this is the only time in the New Testament when someone came to Jesus of Nazareth to ask for help, and expressed doubt. We remember the leper: "Lord, if thou wilt, thou canst make me clean"; the ruler about his daughter: "Speak the word only and she will be healed"; and the woman with the issue of blood: "If I could only touch the hem of His garment": but this man comes saying: "If thou canst do any thing." I believe the doubt of this harassed father was generated by his disappointment in the fact the disciples could not do anything. The impotent disciples caused doubt in the mind of the father, a doubt that went so far he even doubted the Lord. This is something we should think about soberly. Think of the spectacle in the world of a powerless church: a church that does not make any difference to people, has an adverse effect upon people. I am especially concerned about the effect it has upon outsiders and upon young people. If the church is one that goes through the motions – with activities going on – and nothing happening, that will incline people to doubt everything. People will not only doubt the church, but they will, in time, doubt the minister, and they will doubt the Lord and they will doubt the Bible.

But this man came. He needed help badly and he would take it in any way if he could possibly get it. "Jesus said unto him, If thou canst believe, all things are possible to him that believeth" (Mark 9:23). This is impressive. Jesus of Nazareth stopped him in his tracks, and challenged his doubt right there. Unbelief must be dealt with first. No doubt much that is ineffectual is the result of not believing, and many activities go along with no consequences because the people did not expect anything. We must remember that without faith it is impossible to please Him and so, when the man was confronted this way with this challenge he gave expression to a classic utterance: "And straightway the father of the child cried out, and said with tears, Lord, I believe; help thou mine unbelief" (Mark 9:24).

When one says he believes, it is like saying he is swallowing. He may not swallow all there is, but he is not rejecting any part of what he has in his mouth. All that is within reach he will take and that is the way this man was. He would believe everything he could; if there was more he needed to believe he was willing to believe that, too, even if he needed help for it. My believing can be enhanced if I know more about what there is to believe. Sometimes people ask: how would one become a believer and be saved? We will say by faith. But what do we mean by faith? We say: "If you believe." But if you believe what? The fact is you can believe more or less; if you believe more you will be more blessed, and if you believe less you will be less blessed. I am satisfied that the central thing is to believe in the Lord Jesus Christ. But when you believe in Him, what do you believe in Him for? What do you expect of Him?

It may be a person believes Jesus died for his sins. That would be wonderful, for it is true. But what else? He may believe Christ carried his sins away. And that is grand! It will give him peace in his heart. But what else does he believe? You might ask: could there be anything else? So far believing has brought only forgiveness and cleansing, but now what? Does he believe Christ will come and be with him? That He is raised from the dead and is now in the presence of God, praying for him? Does he believe Christ is sending the Holy Spirit into his heart and He will guide him?

This is why we read and study the Bible: the better to understand about the Lord Jesus Christ. I can always start with this: I am to be forgiven, thank the Lord. I am to be delivered, praise the Lord. I am to be filled with the Holy Spirit, glory to His Name. And I am to be led, that will humble me. All of these things come in succession. It is possible that any time one could stop for less than all.

> When Jesus saw that the people came running together, he rebuked the foul spirit, saying unto him, Thou dumb and deaf spirit, I charge thee, come out of him, and enter no more into him. And the spirit cried, and rent him sore, and came out of him: and he was as one dead; insomuch that many said, He is dead. But Jesus took him by the hand, and lifted him up; and he arose. And when he was come into the house, his disciples asked him privately, Why could not we cast him out? And he said unto them, This kind can come forth by nothing, but by prayer and fasting (Mark 9:25-29).

Some of the other Gospels express it differently. Mark here is kind: this is all he says. These men wanted to serve, and their lack of power must have troubled them; the Master indicated that if they were to devote themselves to prayer and fasting they would have had more power in prayer and would have been more effectual in their service.

Chapter 38

TEACHING THE DISCIPLES

(Mark 9:30-48)

We can learn much from reading how Jesus of Nazareth dealt with His disciples because the whole matter of walking with Him was new to them as it may be new to us. He needed to teach them, and this He did.

> And they departed thence, and passed through Galilee; and he would not that any man should know it. For he taught his disciples, and said unto them, The Son of man is delivered into the hands of men, and they shall kill him; and after that he is killed, he shall rise the third day. But they understood not that saying, and were afraid to ask him (Mark 9:30-32).

Does that seem strange? Perhaps His prediction seems simple to us because for over 1900 years all the world has known that Christ Jesus died on the cross. And it has been preached that He rose again. We need to put ourselves in the place of those disciples. They had walked with Jesus of Nazareth, and they had seen the remarkable things He had done. They had heard things from Him and had seen things in Him that were beyond anything they could have expected. Now He told them the Son of man would be delivered into the hands of men, and they would kill Him. "And after that he is killed, he shall rise the third day." They simply could not grasp the plain truth of that statement.

There are times when a believer keeps silent. I may know something it would not be wise to tell. Integrity does not require that everything be told to everyone.

> And he came to Capernaum: and being in the house he asked them, What was it that ye disputed among yourselves by the way? (Mark 9:33).

I am intrigued by that because the Lord knew what was in every man's heart and He knew what they had been saying, but He wanted them to admit it. The word "dispute" means argued about. What did you argue about among yourselves?

> But they held their peace: for by the way they had disputed among themselves, who should be the greatest. And he sat down, and called the twelve, and saith unto them, If any man desire to be first, the same shall be last of all, and servant of all. And he took a child, and set him in the midst of them: and when he had taken him in his arms, he said unto them, Whosoever shall receive one of such children in my name, receiveth me: and whosoever shall receive me, receiveth not me, but him that sent me (Mark 9:34-37).

The child He used as an illustration was young enough to be taken up in arms. When He says "except ye be as little children" He means "as babies that are carried in the arms," and we know what they are like. Such children believe what you say. This is the way we should be with the Lord.

Interest in personal status is normal, not childish. Jesus of Nazareth did not rebuke them for this natural interest; He did not say there was anything wrong about desiring to excel, but He guided them into a wise application of their desire. Did they really want to excel? Then here is how to do it: go to the bottom of the list. Desiring to be first is not evil but seeking it by scrambling for the top spot is foolish and unwise. It is not attained by sophistication but by being childlike.

> And John answered him, saying, Master, we saw one casting out devils in thy name, and he followeth not us: and we forbade him, because he followeth not us. But Jesus said, Forbid him not: for there is no man which shall do a miracle in my name, that can lightly speak evil of me. For he that is not against us is on our part (Mark 9:38-40).

I must keep humbly in mind that no matter what denomination I may belong to, all those in other denominations have open access to the Lord just as I have. This is very important in its bearing on our attitudes toward others who may be different from us. I would like to underscore the Lord's words, "forbid him not." Don't do it. Don't say something against another person because he promotes the gospel in a different way. So far as other people in other churches are concerned, leave them alone. All those who speak of the Lord Jesus as Lord will not do anything lightly against Him.

> For whosoever shall give you a cup of water to drink in my name, because ye belong to Christ, verily I say unto you, he shall not lose his reward. And whosoever shall offend one of these little ones that believe in me, it is better for him that a millstone were hanged about his neck, and he were cast into the sea (Mark 9:41-42).

That is a terribly strong statement. When I first became a believer I read the Bible closely to find out exactly what Jesus Christ had said, and this shocked me. It is so easy to think, because we speak of "the lowly Jesus so gentle and mild," that He would never have anything hard to say about anyone. We could not make a bigger mistake. He is the Lord. This is the world God made, and people whom God made are hurt in it, and people are destroyed. I do not understand all about it but I know enough to simply hold my peace when it comes to questioning the ways of God.

". . . and whosoever shall offend one of these little ones." Who are these little ones? Are they those who are just beginners in the gospel? They may not have had the privilege of joining your church, they may not belong to your company, and they may not have had your special treatment in doctrine. But they are little ones. They are babes. They are in the loving arms of the living Lord. He is holding them, and they are trusting in Him. They do not act as we want them to act, and thus we are inclined to criticize them; but He says, "Don't do it."

Could this be true of a preacher? Could this be true of a professor? Could this be true of anyone who talks about the gospel? If I should talk about the gospel in such a way that I cause a beginning person to stumble, I have stepped on dangerous ground.

> And if thy hand offend thee, cut it off: it is better for thee to enter into life maimed, than having two hands to go into hell, into the fire that never shall be quenched: where their worm dieth not, and the fire is not quenched (Mark 9:43-44).

Those are words of the Lord Jesus Christ. We have never heard anything like them. He is speaking of any person being a stumbling block, causing the little ones to falter. Be careful that you do not disturb the faith of the little ones: Almighty God watches over them in a special way.

When He says, "If thy hand offend thee, cut it off" it may seem rather sharp; but have you not heard something like this: "If any man will be my disciple, let him deny himself, take up his cross and follow me? Have you not heard of being crucified with Christ? Yet, nevertheless you live, because you are believing in the Lord Jesus Christ. Being crucified with Him would be just a little more total than having the hand cut off but what this means is: I am going to deny myself the liberty of action. I am not going to allow myself to do a thing or say a thing that will hinder or hurt anyone. This is a very serious and important passage. We find that uniformity is not demanded, as we saw earlier. They do not all have to be alike but unity is in Christ. Here are some of the most severe utterances by Jesus of Nazareth showing His personal concern for the little ones, and the responsibility of all who deal with them.

Chapter 39

RICH YOUNG RULER

(Mark 10:1-27)

As we continue our study in Mark we see that the Pharisees posed a question to Jesus of Nazareth with the idea of confusing Him. They were going to draw attention to something Moses did which seems to be in conflict with what the law requires.

> And the Pharisees came to him, and asked him, Is it lawful for a man to put away his wife? tempting him. And he answered and said unto them, What did Moses command you? And they said, Moses suffered to write a bill of divorcement, and to put her away. And Jesus answered and said unto them, For the hardness of your heart he wrote you this precept. But from the beginning of the creation God made them male and female. For this cause shall a man leave his father and mother, and cleave to his wife; and they twain shall be one flesh: so then they are no more twain, but one flesh. What therefore God hath joined together, let not man put asunder (Mark 10:2-9).

This is the way the Lord Jesus answered their question. He explained why Moses had given permission for any man to put away his wife.

In posing this question the Pharisees were putting it up to Jesus of Nazareth to explain why Moses would permit divorce in view of the emphasis of the law on one husband and one wife. He explained why Moses gave this permission: namely, for the hardness of their hearts he wrote this precept. This leaves the whole problem of divorce wide open even today. I think in all fairness we could ask this question: would there not be hardness of heart today? And what does all of this seem to say? It seems to say that under certain circumstances divorce will take place.

To my mind this is as if you were to ask what is the physical contour, the normal outline of a person's body, how many arms would he have? Normally, he would have two arms, but if in dire circumstances one should be amputated it would not mean the man would die. So it would be with reference to this. Despite the planned pattern for a man's body in which he has two legs, it is nonetheless true that if one were amputated the man could still live. This seems to me to be about how the Lord answered this question. There are many other questions that come to mind, but I will not go into them at this time, except to alert you; I want to make you mindful of the thought that practical circumstances can make a difference in the meaning of a person's conduct.

> And they brought young children to him, that he should touch them: and his disciples rebuked those that brought them. But when Jesus saw it, he was much displeased, and said unto them, Suffer the little children to come unto me, and forbid them not: for of such is the kingdom of God. Verily I say unto you, Whosoever shall not receive the kingdom of God as a little child, he shall not enter therein. And he took them up in his arms, put his hands upon them, and blessed them (Mark 10:13-16).

This is one of the sweetest passages in Scripture and one everyone should keep in mind. The meaning is plain.

The story of the rich young ruler is one of the best known events in the record of the life of Jesus of Nazareth. It is not surprising that a person would want to be blessed of God: that makes sense. Anyone would want to succeed, to get ahead. No one wants to be found at fault and no one wants to be a failure. I do not even want to be punished; in fact, I could say with many, if there is any balm in Gilead, any way to escape loss, I am all for it. In this way we can appreciate this young ruler when he came to Jesus of Nazareth.

> And when he was gone forth into the way, there came one running, and kneeled to him, and asked him, Good Master, what shall I do that I may inherit eternal life? And Jesus said unto him, Why callest thou me good? there is none good but one, that is, God. Thou knowest the commandments, Do not commit adultery, Do not kill, Do not steal, Do not bear false witness, Defraud not, Honor thy father and mother. And he answered and said unto him, Master, all these have I observed from my youth. Then Jesus beholding him loved him, and said unto him, One thing thou lackest: go thy way, sell whatsoever thou hast, and give to the poor, and thou shalt have treasure in heaven: and come, take up the cross, and follow me. And he was sad at that saying, and went away grieved: for he had great possessions (Mark 10:17-22).

There is so much to be learned in this event. "What shall I do?" This was a natural approach, but can you understand that doing everything as it should be done is not the way to be saved? When the rich young ruler said he had observed all these things from his youth up, I do not think he necessarily claimed he had never made a mistake or that he had never in any way sinned; but I do think he meant he had followed through as the law prescribed in the event he sinned. He was always of a frame of mind to confess his sin and to bring a sacrifice to God. That would be keeping the law and doing all the things he should do.

It is significant to note that Jesus beholding him loved him: I think this was in a special way, not just the general love the Son of God would have for men everywhere. Evidently the young man was genuinely sincere. Then the Master told him, "One thing thou lackest. Go thy way, sell whatsoever thou hast, (which is, transfer the ownership of your possessions) give to the poor (use everything you have for the sake of people who do not have it) then come, take up the cross and follow me."

In these words the significant phrase is "take up the cross." This is not a matter of adjusting myself to my problems; it is not a matter of meekly and humbly accepting my lot, whatever that may be. Taking up the cross will be doing for myself what Jesus of Nazareth did for Himself when He went to the cross, namely: committing myself to self-denial. In another place it is recorded: "If any man will come after me, let him deny himself, and take up his cross, and follow me" (Matt. 16:24). When He had told him this the young man was sad at the saying, and went away grieved for he had great possessions. At that point Jesus of Nazareth turned to teach His disciples:

> And Jesus looked round about, and saith unto his disciples, How hardly shall they that have riches enter into the kingdom of God! And the disciples were astonished at his words. But Jesus answereth again, and saith unto them, Children, how hard is it for them that trust in riches to enter into the kingdom of God! It is easier for a camel to go through the eye of a needle, than for a rich man to enter into the kingdom of God. And they were astonished out of measure, saying among themselves, Who then can be saved? And Jesus looking upon them saith, With men it is impossible, but not with God: for with God all things are possible (Mark 10:23-27).

At this point I would like to share what my own reading has uncovered, especially about the days in which these things occurred. It seems that the phrase "the eye of the needle" was the term given to a small gate in the wall; we might call it the pedestrian gate. You remember that the cities in those days were walled around to keep out bandits and hostile forces. There was always a big gate for the caravans to go through. People riding camels and coming in processions would go through that big gate in the wall. At sunrise it would be opened but at sundown that gate was closed. There was beside the big gate a small gate through which the pedestrians could pass. This gate, although small and intended only for persons on foot to go through, could accommodate a camel; but it would be a tight squeeze, as we would say. It would appear this gate was lower than the height of a camel and narrow. A camel could squeeze through but it would have to do it like this: the camel would have to unload all his baggage and he would have to get on his knees, then he could squirm through the gate. And that is precisely the way it would be with the rich man.

No wonder they asked, who, then, could be saved? It will help to remember that riches is not always money. Riches may include personality, education, culture, opportunity and everything that gives one an advantage over others. If you have an advantage over other people in any way, it will be difficult for you to come into the kingdom of God because riches can so easily corrupt. They make us self-satisfied, self-confident; and if we have riches we think we are better than others.

There is a way to handle riches. Regardless of what it is: whether you have education, a good family, or whatever it is, there is a way in which you can handle riches so that they will not corrupt you. Use them for the poor. And who are the poor? The people who do not have the advantages you have. Deny self and yield to the Lord. In that way a smart man, by being humble, can enter into the kingdom of God. A rich man with money, by being generous, can enter into the kingdom of God. A cultured person, by being kind and thoughtful to the poor and to the uncultured, can enter into the kingdom of God. These are the conditions that will help to prepare a person to accept the Lord.

Chapter 40

SECRET OF PREEMINENCE

(Mark 10:32-52)

> And they were in the way going up to Jerusalem; and Jesus went before them: and they were amazed; and as they followed, they were afraid. And he took again the twelve, and began to tell them what things should happen unto him (Mark 10:32).

This is a continuation of the report of Jesus of Nazareth teaching His disciples. When I read "and they were amazed" I have an open mind about it. What was it that amazed them? It seems to me it may have been the attitude of the people round about. "And as they followed, they were afraid." There must have been something threatening, something sinister in the attitude of the people toward the Lord. As the disciples went with Him one of the reasons they were amazed might well be that, normally speaking, Jesus of Nazareth was welcome anywhere He went — but here He was faced with an unusual reaction and the disciples were afraid. They feared what might happen.

> And he took again the twelve, and began to tell them what things should happen unto him, saying, Behold, we go up to Jerusalem; and the Son of man shall be delivered unto the chief priests, and unto the scribes; and they shall condemn him to death, and shall deliver him to the Gentiles: and they shall mock him, and shall scourge him, and shall spit upon him, and shall kill him: and the third day he shall rise again (Mark 10:32-34).

All this was set out before them. Jesus of Nazareth knew His career would have a violent end and He began to prepare His disciples for this shocking event. At this point we should make the general observation, nothing is gained by ignoring unpleasant prospects. We could say you will not get anywhere by shutting your eyes to what is going to happen. Especially is this true, if some of the prospects are unpleasant. If we know beforehand they are unpleasant, we may keep that in mind; and so this can be a corrective to our natural disposition. Normally speaking, it is a common human trait that we do not want to look at coming trouble. If we know there is going to be trouble, we do not want to think about it now. It is unwise to think we can handle trouble by ignoring it in the hope it will go away. Jesus of Nazareth not only told them about the distress to come; He brought out the fact it was all leading to a certain promise.

> Behold, we go up to Jerusalem; and the Son of man shall be delivered unto the chief priests, and unto the scribes; and they shall condemn him to death, and shall deliver him to the Gentiles: and they shall mock him, and shall scourge him, and shall spit upon him, and shall kill him, and the third day he shall rise again (Mark 10:33-34).

Certainly that will be trouble but beyond the trouble there is blessing. Certainly there is distress but beyond the distress there is glory. There is one thing true about believing in the Lord Jesus Christ: it will come out well. It may be that in the world we will have tribulation but we can be of good cheer, He has overcome the world. We put our trust in Him, and we are going on through.

> And James and John, the sons of Zebedee, come unto him, saying, Master, we would that thou shouldest do for us whatsoever we shall desire. And he said unto them, What would ye that I should do for you? They said unto him, Grant unto us that we may sit, one on thy right hand, and the other on thy left hand, in thy glory. But Jesus said unto them. Ye know not what ye ask: can ye drink of the cup that I drink of? and be baptized with the baptism that I am baptized with? And they said unto him, We can. And Jesus said unto them, Ye shall indeed drink of the cup that I drink of; and with the baptism that I am baptized withal shall ye be baptized: but to sit on my right hand and on my left hand is not mine to give; but it shall be given to them for whom it is prepared. And when the ten heard it, they began to be much displeased with James and John (Mark 10:35-41).

This all sounds quite human, doesn't it? James and John were ambitious. They wanted to be assured an important place. It is conceivable they may not even have analyzed their motives too closely. I am not real sure they were thinking only of their own prestige. It is quite possible they were wanting only to be close to Him. In any case, they wanted more than it was possible for them to have. Not only were they ambitious; they were dedicated, sincere servants of the Lord who would like to amount to something in the Lord. They wanted, however, more than it was possible for them to have. They were not rebuked for their zeal because they wanted to be near the Lord, but they were taught a better way.

> But Jesus called them to him, and saith unto them, Ye know that they which are accounted to rule over the Gentiles exercise lordship over them; and their great ones exercise authority upon them. But so shall it not be among you:

> but whosoever will be great among you, shall be your minister: and whosoever of you will be the chiefest, shall be servant of all. For even the Son of man came not to be ministered unto, but to minister, and to give his life a ransom for many (Mark 10:42-45).

This is profoundly significant because it points out the difference between the kingdom of God in the Lord Jesus Christ and other kingdoms among men. The principal difference to be noted is the essential drive that marks these two kingdoms. Among the Gentiles this is the striking characteristic: the leader, the ruler, the great one, shows his authority by commanding others and demanding his own prestige. He is given praise and adulation. People bow down to him. He is the great one. But among the people of God the leader is the servant of all. It is important to have in mind that "whosoever will be great among you, shall be your minister: and whosoever of you will be the chiefest, shall be servant of all." Jesus of Nazareth did not hesitate to urge His followers to keep in mind He is the One who moves directly to serve, by giving Himself. That is what Christ did, and if the Spirit of Christ is in me, that is how I will be moved. There is nothing wrong with wanting to be a chief servant: the Lord did not criticize that, but He directed how to do it. The way to serve is to be humble.

After this the account turns to a different line of thought. It is significant to note how these are put together in the record. I am inclined to feel that Mark was led by the Holy Spirit to put these together in just this way in this one series. The discussion about eminence is followed by this instance of the one born blind who came asking for help. The blind man was persistent; others tried to discourage him but his need was prompting his earnest persistence. The Son of God was more gracious than people expected Him to be on that day.

> And Jesus stood still, and commanded him to be called. And they call the blind man, saying unto him, Be of good comfort, rise; he calleth thee. And he, casting away his garment, rose, and came to Jesus. And Jesus answered and said unto him, What wilt thou that I should do unto thee? The blind man said unto him, Lord, that I might receive my sight. And Jesus said unto him, Go thy way; thy faith hath made thee whole. And immediately he received his sight, and followed Jesus in the way (Mark 10:49-52).

The blind man was in need, and when he came before Jesus of Nazareth he expressed his need. Did you notice that the Son of God, who knew everything, certainly knew what was the matter with this man: but this man needed to say what he wanted. This is one more instance of the remarkable grace and power of the living Lord Jesus Christ.

Chapter 41

THE TRIUMPHAL ENTRY

(Mark 11:1-10)

All the truth about Jesus of Nazareth that was to be revealed was revealed in something done. He did not appear in person as so different from other human beings. There was nothing to be seen when you looked at Him that would reveal who He was. Words of description and words of explanation would never be enough. We are reminded that actions speak louder than words. The ways of God are different. Human talk can never make it clear what you really mean when you talk about the ways of God. This must be demonstrated. "My thoughts are not your thoughts; neither are your ways my ways, saith the Lord."

When we think about Jesus of Nazareth and look to see in Him the King of Kings it is probable we would expect to see a grand display of some kind. Yet this is not what happened.

> And when they came nigh to Jerusalem, unto Bethphage and Bethany, at the mount of Olives, he sendeth forth two of his disciples, and saith unto them, Go your way into the village over against you: and as soon as ye be entered into it, ye shall find a colt tied, whereon never man sat; loose him, and bring him. And if any man say unto you, Why do ye this? say ye that the Lord hath need of him; and straightway he will send him hither. And they went their way, and found the colt tied by the door without in a place where two ways met; and they loose him. And certain of them that stood there said unto them, What do ye, loosing the colt? And they said unto them even as Jesus had commanded: and they let them go. And they brought the colt to Jesus, and cast their garments on him; and he sat upon him. And many spread their garments in the way: and others cut down branches off the trees, and strewed them in the way. And they that went before, and they that followed, cried, saying, Hosanna; Blessed is he that cometh in the name of the Lord: Blessed be the kingdom of our father David, that cometh in the name of the Lord: Hosanna in the highest (Mark 11:1-10).

This is the simple straightforward account of what happened. I cannot fully explain what we should understand or what we should think about how that colt was obtained. When He said,

"Say ye that the Lord hath need of him; and straightway he will send him hither," I have often wondered how that was arranged. Does that mean Jesus of Nazareth had talked to this man beforehand, or does it mean He knew the owner's heart and mind would be such that he would simply say, "Take him." It leaves me wondering; I am not worried about it, but I am recognizing there is more here than is written. They brought the colt to Jesus and cast their garments on Him. With all the excitement that must have been there can you recognize a description of the beginning of something like a procession or a parade? Can you see how it would be with the streets filled with people shouting and singing "Hosanna in the highest"?

Even though a person may not have been reared on a farm, I believe anyone could understand this would be very exciting for any animal. If a colt were taken into a town and a large crowd of people shouted and threw palm branches on the street in front of him, don't you think such activity would disturb any colt? Of course, you have in mind this was a colt on which never man had sat. That means he was not broken in to ride; he was an unbroken colt. The people had no saddle; they just put their garments on the colt for Him to sit on. Jesus went down the street riding on this colt in that crowd. What an astonishing experience.

It was my privilege to serve for a length of time in the army. My unit was attached to a cavalry regiment. There were occasions when we rode horseback in parades. The infantrymen had to walk on foot and the artillery rode on their wagons but the cavalrymen rode on horses. One of the few thrills we had in the service was to ride horseback in a parade. Some horses, even though they were old and experienced, could not be taken to a parade. They became so nervous it was impossible to control them. Even so, the event was always exciting; and I suppose that is one reason why it comes to mind.

Jesus of Nazareth rode on that colt; and the colt went right down the street, apparently not upset by any disturbance. I draw your attention to this because I think we have revealed here an intimation of the nature of the kingdom of God – of the kingdom of the Lord Jesus Christ. We remember promises in the Old Testament that "...the cow and the bear shall feed; their young ones shall lie down together: and the lion shall eat straw like the ox. And the sucking child shall play on the hole of the asp, and the weaned child shall put his hand on the cockatrice' den. They shall not hurt nor destroy in all my holy mountain" (Isa. 11:7-9). All these would indicate a certain control over nature. There are other ways this is emphasized in

Scripture but I bring it to your mind in this instance because I think it predicts something: the natural disposition of the natural creatures will be controlled by Christ. There is no indication in the account that would indicate outward coercion or control: that colt was controlled by Christ in such a way that he did exactly what he was supposed to do. How this was done will remain obscure, but that it happened is notable and to His glory.

Let me carry this line of thought a little further: because I am a believer I could be expected to walk with Christ and to obey Him. Do you realize I have a problem? I walk in my flesh (in the old man) and my flesh is just as independent as any colt. In my flesh I am inclined to do as I please. As I walk with the Lord the flesh in me is constantly inclined to do my own will. It is the common problem for any person walking with the Lord to bring his flesh into obedience. If you have lived any length of time as a believer, you will know you cannot do it in your own strength. This little incident reveals clearly you will not have to do it in your own strength; it will be God working in you to will and to do of His good pleasure. It will be "Christ in you." Just as it happened with that colt it can happen in anyone who believes.

> But if the Spirit of him that raised up Jesus from the dead dwell in you, he that raised up Christ from the dead shall also quicken your mortal bodies by his Spirit that dwelleth in you. Therefore, brethren, we are debtors, not to the flesh, to live after the flesh. For if ye live after the flesh, ye shall die: but if ye through the Spirit do mortify the deeds of the body, ye shall live. For as many as are led by the Spirit of God, they are the sons of God (Rom. 8:11-14).

Just as that colt was controlled by Jesus of Nazareth, so my body can be led by the Spirit of the Lord in me. This is true freedom: no contention, no strife, no hanging back on my part, no fighting against the reins or against the rope on my part; but walking along with Him willingly, totally committed to the living God. Living the spiritual life in Christ means denying the self unto death, and receiving from God the Holy Spirit; so that I am inwardly led by the Spirit of Christ. The very body I have, the very human nature I have, is so affected by His presence I am inclined to walk His way. We remember how He put it: "A body hast thou prepared me . . . Lo, I come to do thy will, O God" (Heb. 10:5-7). I trust you see the picture and get the idea that it is possible for us, believing in the Lord Jesus Christ, to find the Spirit of God will control our beings in such a way we will be minded to walk with Him in the fullness of our heart, without pressure or strain or stress because we want to – because He has won us over to Himself.

Chapter 42

EXERCISING AUTHORITY

(Mark 11:11-33)

Many seem to think Jesus of Nazareth was always gentle and mild. They feel the harsh judgments in the Old Testament are now overruled, because they have been outdated. We are not to expect anything like that any more. And for some this creates a real problem. There seems to be some conflict here. It is like an apparent conflict between the harsh facts of life all around us and the popular notion of a sweet mild Jesus. How can you account for things being as rough as they are if God is always kind? And how can you account for things being so terrible as they can be if Jesus of Nazareth is on the throne? In fact many feel that hell cannot be real because Jesus Christ is the truth. Such thoughts as that indicate the persons thinking them really do not know what the Scriptures say.

The Scriptures record that Jesus of Nazareth talked more about hell than anyone in the New Testament. In a recent chapter we noted He said it would have been better for some if they had never been born or a millstone had been put about their neck and they had been dropped in the depth of the sea. Even so, in spite of the fact that we have these glimpses, these traces in the Scriptures of the fact that the awful things, the hard things, are actually under the will of God, some find it hard to believe Jesus Christ would ever be stern. They find it hard to accept Christ Jesus would ever be hard. Our portion of Scripture today will note two examples.

In Mark chapter 11 verses 11 to 33 there are two incidents for our notice. Interestingly enough in each case there is first one part in which a certain act is performed and then later in the text there is an explanation of it. For instance the first one is in verses 12 to 14 and then 20 to 26, and then the second one from verses 15 to 19 and then verses 29 to 33. The first one has to do with cursing the fig tree – dealing with nature. The second has to do with cleansing the Temple – dealing with people. Let us read these and open our hearts and minds to see what the Scriptures reveal.

> And on the morrow, when they were come from Bethany, he was hungry: and seeing a fig tree afar off having leaves, he came, if haply he might find anything thereon: and when he came to it, he found nothing but leaves; for the time of figs was not yet. And Jesus answered and said unto it, No man eat fruit of thee hereafter for ever. And his disciples heard it (Mark 11:12-14).

That is a simple declaration. There is no indication of His feelings. It does not mean to say He was disappointed, or surprised, or angry. Nothing like that. It was simply a straightforward statement that there was to be no more food eaten from that tree.

> And in the morning, as they passed by, they saw the fig tree dried up from the roots. And Peter calling to remembrance saith unto him, Master, behold, the fig tree which thou cursedst is withered away. And Jesus answering saith unto them, Have faith in God. For verily I say unto you, That whosoever shall say unto this mountain, Be thou removed, and be thou cast into the sea; and shall not doubt in his heart, but shall believe that those things which he saith shall come to pass; he shall have whatsoever he saith. Therefore I say unto you, What things soever ye desire, when ye pray, believe that ye receive them, and ye shall have them. And when ye stand praying, forgive, if ye have aught against any: that your Father also which is in heaven may forgive you your trespasses. But if ye do not forgive, neither will your Father which is in heaven forgive your trespasses (Mark 11:20-26).

This is the interpretation Jesus of Nazareth gave, and it amounts to an astounding doctrine. There is no doubt many will stumble at these words: "Have faith in God." What does this mean? This does not mean that I go ahead and make my plans, or select some one thing I want, and then I go ahead and work on it and turn to God and say, "Come and endorse what I have done." That is not having faith in God. Having faith in God means I believe that what God has promised, He can and He will perform, not that I can do what I want to do, and then ask God to bless it. That would be foolish. It is not any capricious or willful desire of mine that can be sure of blessing. It is doubtless true this is so often the case, and so many of us live that way.

Day in and day out we live with all kinds of desires and yearnings and longings in our hearts. I am sure when we open our eyes in the morning and start functioning for the day there are things we want right then. There will be some things we are not going to get. We may start feeling bad right now in that we are not going to get today what we want because we want this and we want that. So we turn to God and ask Him for it. When the Scripture says, "What things soever ye desire," this does not mean whatsoever things we desire out of our own heart. But of that which God has promised to do, whatsoever things of those that we would choose, we should ask and we will get it. When I come to pray the first question I should ask is, "What has God promised for me today?" And then, in connection with thinking of what else He has said, I may keep this in mind: have I forgiven everyone? Am I holding a grudge? Is there anything today that would disqualify me?

One thing that will disqualify me from getting answers to my prayers is ignorance of His will. If I do not know what He has promised, if I do not have any idea what I am going to believe, I need not expect His blessing. I may want to believe my own ideas, but that is not what the Bible encourages me to do. If I do not know what He has said, if I do not know His will, if I do not keep in mind His purpose, then there is nothing for me to believe. In the second place, another thing that would disqualify me is my being unforgiving: as when there are some things I still hold against certain people. Now this is the hard, unshakeable truth.

> And they come to Jerusalem: and Jesus went into the temple, and began to cast out them that sold and bought in the temple, and overthrew the tables of the moneychangers, and the seats of them that sold doves; and would not suffer that any man should carry any vessel through the temple. And he taught, saying unto them, Is it not written, My house shall be called of all nations the house of prayer? but ye have made it a den of thieves. And the scribes and chief priests heard it, and sought how they might destroy him: for they feared him, because all the people were astonished at his doctrine. And when even was come, he went out of the city (Mark 11:15-19).

This is a widely known incident, this occasion when Jesus of Nazareth cast out the moneychangers. Let us not read into this more than is there, but let us not skip any part of it. Let's just see exactly what it means. Selling animals for sacrifice in the temple area was a normal practice in Jerusalem. Strangers coming from afar and wanting to bring animals into the temple to sacrifice them would not bring their own sheep and their own goats. They would not bring their doves with them from long distances, but would buy them locally. And because they would buy them locally, the men who had them for sale would naturally want to make sales so they kept moving in closer and closer to the temple itself. The temple was not just one building, one structure, but a complex of buildings like a university. There were courtyards where they would bring their cattle and their sheep for sale. The moneychangers were there because these worshipers came with their own money from other countries. Because their money was not local money, they would have to get it exchanged. The moneychangers were there to provide the money that was needed. In discounting the foreign money they would be making money on the exchange. These merchants, eager to sell their animals and exchange the money, had moved into the temple area making a common practice of doing their business there. Moving these operations into the temple was a practical procedure. They wanted to make as much money as they possibly could. But this impinged upon the sanctity of the temple.

These practices among the merchants reveal an important truth. In doing what is practical, people can actually profane the holy. A person can bring sacred matters down to ordinary levels by being just practical; and the Lord will sharply judge those who profane His worship. In the latter part of this chapter it is made clear that Jesus of Nazareth yielded His authority to judge to no man (Mark 11:27-33). He was actually the Lord of Lords and the King of Kings. In this study we have noted that Jesus of Nazareth exercised authority over natural processes in controlling them and disposing of those that were not suitable to Him. In the second place He had a zeal for the glory of His Father in the matter of worship. He resisted and condemned any tendency to make the practice of worship a practical problem, bringing it down to routine affairs, and mixing the things that were holy with the things that were of this earth, which are profane. In both areas the action of Jesus of Nazareth was drastic and hard. What He did in His zeal was done to glorify His Father.

Chapter 43

PARABLE OF THE VINEYARD

(Mark 12:1-12)

Every human being lives in this world which was made by God and kept by God. Every human being who ever lived has done so by the grace of God. Man is totally dependent upon God for all things including every opportunity before him. Many things he needs are provided free. He has a certain freedom of choice – he can choose as he will. But man is responsible to God; he must render an account for that which has been given to him. "To whom much is given, much shall be required." Some persons have been given great advantages and for this they must answer for the way they have dealt with them. In the time of Jesus of Nazareth the Jews were the fortunate people. Their leaders were also fortunate. They had the Old Testament and the traditions of Israel, and to them Christ Jesus came.

> And he began to speak unto them by parables. A certain man planted a vineyard, and set a hedge about it, and digged a place for the winevat, and built a tower, and let it out to husbandmen, and went into a far country. And at the season he sent to the husbandmen a servant, that he might receive from the husbandmen of the fruit of the vineyard. And they caught him, and beat him, and sent him away empty. And again he sent unto them another servant; and at him they cast stones, and wounded him in the head, and sent him away shamefully handled. And again he sent another; and him they killed, and many others; beating some, and killing some. Having yet therefore one son, his well-beloved, he sent him also last unto them, saying, They will reverence my son. But those husbandmen said among themselves, This is the heir; come, let us kill him, and the inheritance shall be ours. And they took him, and killed him, and cast him out of the vineyard. What shall therefore the lord of the vineyard do? he will come and destroy the husbandmen, and will give the vineyard unto others. And have ye not read this scripture; The stone which the builders rejected is become the head of the corner: this was the Lord's doing, and it is marvelous in our eyes? And they sought to lay hold on him, but feared the people: for they knew that he had spoken the parable against them: and they left him, and went their way (Mark 12:1-12).

The message of this parable is rather sharp. In many ways it reveals a stern difference from many of the things we have heard in the gracious gospel of the Lord Jesus Christ. The truth presented here is vitally important. Certain benefits are given to certain persons; not to everyone. Everyone receives something. Anyone who has the gift of life has received something. But some people are even more fortunate; by comparison with others they are favored (think of the blessings we Americans enjoy in this country). We may have many complaints and misgivings about our government, and we may feel free to criticize in many ways; but of all the countries in the world I wonder if there are any of us who would wish to be anywhere else. My own sober judgment is that this is the most blessed place to live in the whole world.

In our culture, the traditions people have and the ideas people have almost defy description. With us the public is encouraged to care for the aged and children and to help the sick. We have various emphases that we take for granted amongst us, in helping the poor and the unfortunate. By and large, all over the country the gospel is being preached; churches are to be found in every town. The name of Christ is known and the promise of the gospel is known. Whether we respond or not does not alter the fact that we have been given a great advantage.

In this parable the owner looks for a report of the record of what has been done with what had been given. This prompts us to think of the evangelists who are preaching the gospel all over our country and elsewhere in the world? What have people done with the message? What is being done by parents in bringing their children to Sunday school? How careful are the churches as to what is being taught? The majority of preachers are dedicated persons who are seeking to help other people know about God. All these advantages constitute a definite call to come to God. Unquestionably we are responsible to Him for what we do with the privileges we have enjoyed. Messengers bringing the Word of God have been sent to us: this includes mothers teaching their children, Sunday school teachers, preachers and evangelists. Books are being written, discussions are being held and activities are being promoted in which the Word of God is being presented. Discussions have been promoted on our campuses in various places, seeking to open up to the people an understanding of what the gospel actually is. All this is being done, and yet widely this witness is being ignored. People have their backs turned to it. It is being scorned in many places and rejected. This should make us very concerned.

What is in store for any person who neglects or who rejects

the gospel of the Lord Jesus Christ? This parable is plain. Many will feel perhaps they have not acted in this whole matter of rejecting the gospel, but did they share in such rejection? Did they accept the gospel? God is calling all men unto Himself, and He works things around to have men turn their attention to Him. He is holding out His hand everywhere to all men.

> Then shall he say also unto them on the left hand, Depart from me, ye cursed, into everlasting fire, prepared for the devil and his angels: for I was an hungered, and ye gave me no meat: I was thirsty, and ye gave me no drink: I was a stranger, and ye took me not in: naked, and ye clothed me not: sick, and in prison, and ye visited me not. Then shall they also answer him, saying, Lord, when saw we thee an hungered, or athirst, or a stranger, or naked, or sick, or in prison, and did not minister unto thee? Then shall he answer them, saying, Verily I say unto you, Inasmuch as ye did it not to one of the least of these, ye did it not to me. And these shall go away into everlasting punishment: but the righteous into life eternal (Matt. 25:41-46).

One would almost wonder, "Did I read that in the Bible? Were those words of the Lord Jesus Christ?" It is all true. We are anxious to encourage people to know the Lord as gracious and merciful, and Almighty God as kind, but sometimes my heart is shaken when I wonder if I am giving the wrong impression.

> For as Jonah was three days and three nights in the whale's belly; so shall the Son of man be three days and three nights in the heart of the earth. The men of Nineveh shall rise in judgment with this generation, and shall condemn it: because they repented at the preaching of Jonah; and, behold, a greater than Jonah is here. The queen of the south shall rise up in the judgment with this generation, and shall condemn it: for she came from the uttermost parts of the earth to hear the wisdom of Solomon; and, behold, a greater than Solomon is here (Matt. 12:40-42).

Perhaps we do not realize that when we ignore what the Sunday school teacher is teaching, when we ignore what our mothers are telling us and what the preachers are preaching to us, we are actually ignoring the Lord Himself. In the last analysis the unbeliever is rejecting Christ, rejecting God, and such rejection is not innocent. A person will not get away with it, even though he says, "I didn't mean any harm." The fact is he didn't mean any good, either. God will actually bring judgment upon those who reject the gospel. Those who do not receive it are rejecting it. Truth which has been rejected by many could be the very basis of the salvation of God. All of this was written for our learning. Our generation is in grave danger of being judged of God for rejecting the call of God.

Chapter 44

ANSWERING OPPOSITION

(Mark 12:13-44)

Jesus of Nazareth was opposed at times and criticized on the basis of false principles. There was no basis for what was being said about Him. Notice this: He not only refused to accept the criticism, He was not affected by what the people said because what they were saying was wrong; but He took time to show the error of their thinking, of their basic premise. The underlying principles which they had accepted as true were actually false.

Mark sets forth the record of a great confrontation when Jesus of Nazareth met the critics, and exposed the fallacies in their ideas in three leading areas.

> And they send unto him certain of the Pharisees and of the Herodians, to catch him in his words. And when they were come, they say unto him, Master, we know that thou art true, and carest for no man: for thou regardest not the person of men, but teachest the way of God in truth: Is it lawful to give tribute to Caesar, or not? Shall we give, or shall we not give? But he, knowing their hypocrisy, said unto them, Why tempt ye me? bring me a penny, that I may see it. And they brought it. And he said unto them, Whose is this image and superscription? And they said unto him, Caesar's. And Jesus answering said unto them, Render to Caesar the things that are Caesar's, and to God the things that are God's. And they marveled at him (Mark 12:13-17).

One of the reasons why they raised the question of paying taxes was that Caesar was a pagan. Should the people of God pay taxes to a pagan government, a government without faith in God? This question was not a proper question because it ignored the truth that the people living in that country already owed the government something.

I do not pay taxes because I believe in what the government is doing: I pay taxes because I live here and I have all of the benefits of this country. I am not paying my taxes because I am supporting a program or approving a procedure or policy. I am paying my taxes because I am using other people's things and I should pay what I owe regardless of who my creditor is.

> Then come unto him the Sadducees, which say there is no resurrection; and they asked him, saying, Master, Moses wrote unto us, If a man's brother die, and leave his wife behind him, and leave no children, that his brother should take his wife, and raise up seed unto his brother. Now there were seven brethren: and the first took a wife, and dying left no seed. And the second took her, and died, neither left he any seed: and the third likewise. And the seven had her, and left no seed: last of all the woman died also. In the resurrection therefore, when they shall rise, whose wife shall she be of them? for the seven had her to wife. And Jesus answering said unto them, Do ye not therefore err, because ye know not the scriptures, neither the power of God? For when they shall rise from the dead, they neither marry, nor are given in marriage; but are as the angels which are in heaven. And as touching the dead, that they rise: have ye not read in the book of Moses, how in the bush God spake unto him, saying, I am the God of Abraham, and the God of Isaac, and the God of Jacob? He is not the God of the dead, but the God of the living: ye therefore do greatly err (Mark 12:18-27).

When we look at this question of the Sadducees we need to notice it is not valid, because it takes an item of scriptural teaching without noting the context in Scripture. They asked Him if it was reasonable to accept the teaching that includes the idea of heaven, because they claimed what is taught about heaven is not practical in this world. He pointed out that in their questioning they were omitting what the Scriptures teach and the power of God. The Scriptures reveal certain aspects of living in heaven when the nature of the believer will be different from what it was when he was alive on earth; and by reason of the supernatural power of God, which will make living in the spirit possible, the reality of heaven is not a matter of question.

The Scriptures refer to Old Testament persons who are considered to be living now. God is the God of Abraham now. This is a rather obscure question and answer, but very real, especially to educated, sophisticated people. When I think about the gospel and it does not sound reasonable to me, is that a proper basis for questioning it? The fact is I might not know enough to be a competent judge. I might not believe enough to understand the Scriptures. If I am going to read the Bible to understand it, I must have in mind all the Bible teaches; and I must have in mind the power of God as set forth in the Bible. Then these things which I read can make sense. Apart from such additional information they would not make sense. When a person says, "That is not reasonable to me," he is not saying anything about the gospel or about the message, he is saying something about himself. If he would open his eyes and look in the right direction he would see far more than he does now.

> And one of the scribes came, and having heard them reasoning together, and perceiving that he had answered them well, asked him, Which is the first commandment of all? (Mark 12:28).

If you will read on through this passage you will find the man asking this question: "What is good, above all else; what is the first great thing that is good in the sight of God?" To lift some one manner of conduct above another is not valid. It is not that this is a good thing to do or that is a good thing to do because the one great principle that matters is the attitude of the heart toward God. What is really good? It is that we get right with God. It is not whether we should spend our money here, or whether we should support that, or whether we should oppose this; the good thing is that we should be yielded to God.

These three questions are classic forms of human error. The first one was a legal question, "What must I do?" What we need to have in mind about this is: I am not free to do as I please: I am under certain obligations and I need to carry those out. The second one is the rational question: "What makes sense?" Here I would say we cannot go by reason, if we are ignorant. If we are ignorant and do not know, reason cannot help; reason will never discover a new thing. Reason can only expose what is in the situation, and if there is nothing there, it cannot be exposed. If I do not know anything I cannot have any reason about it. If I do not understand about the things of God and I do not believe in the things of God, I never in the wide world can find the promises of God reasonable. The third one is what we call ethical: "What is the greatest good?" Nothing is really good if my heart is not right. If my heart is right everything is good. The basic question above all others was then set before them by Jesus of Nazareth: "What think ye of Christ?" Mark reports "the common people heard him gladly" (Mark 12:37).

This portion has two more important truths. Firstly there is a warning about sophisticated leaders. They can deceive. We need to be extremely careful about this. He tells us to beware of the scribes. Secondly He stresses that the valid principle for estimating the size of any gift is proportion. He pointed out the woman who cast the two mites into the treasury. Turning to His disciples, He asked, "Did you see that? Did you see what that woman gave? She gave more than anyone." The "more" is based on comparison with what you have. The quality of service is according to what you can do. The quality of response in every case depends on the circumstances, and the opportunity. The person who can do much is responsible to do much, and the person who can only do a little is not responsible to do more.

Chapter 45

END OF THE WORLD

(Mark 13:1-37)

When we think about God the Creator of all things and the Judge of all the earth, the mind moves on into concern about the end of the world. God is the Creator, Maker and Keeper. He is the Provider, the Judge, and by His grace, He is the Savior. Because all this is true His will is the important factor. What will He do? What is His mind on a particular subject? We understand that Jesus of Nazareth, who was the Son of God, was the express image of God. He knew the mind of His Father, and He could reveal what God had in mind to do. His activity on earth shows the primary interest of Jesus of Nazareth was to reconcile man to God. He came to seek and to save the lost. In His talks, His parables, and especially in personal dealings, He sought to bring souls to God. Some may feel that with the record reading as it does there seems to be almost a lack of interest in this world as such. But this is not true, and we will see that He did have an attitude toward this world that was real.

In Mark 13 we will notice what the Lord had to say about the end of the world. There are several important aspects of the final phase of this world revealed in this chapter. I am always hesitant to undertake identifying details in any vision or any prophecy, and I feel that way about this portion of Scripture. But there are some principles that seem obvious and important. I am sure this is written for our learning upon whom the ends of the world have come.

> And as he went out of the temple, one of his disciples saith unto him, Master, see what manner of stones and what buildings are here! And Jesus answering said unto him, Seest thou these great buildings? there shall not be left one stone upon another, that shall not be thrown down (Mark 13:1-2).

The temple was not just one building; it was a complex of buildings, like a university. When they said, "See what manner of stones," they probably meant that some of those stones had been brought in from great distances. The buildings would probably be built of special material brought to Jerusalem from other parts of the world.

The first direct prediction we have here is that the temple being built right then would be destroyed. That actually happened at the time Jerusalem was destroyed when the Romans besieged the city under Titus. Having had to face the stubborn defense on the part of the Jews the Romans were so enraged they vowed they would not leave one stone upon another. History reports they did try to destroy absolutely the entire city. As a matter of fact, it has been commonly felt that traditionally the portion of the wall left standing in Jerusalem, commonly called the "wailing wall," is probably the only part of the old city still standing. This is where the Jews have gathered throughout all the generations since that time to lament their national desolation before God.

> And as he sat upon the mount of Olives over against the temple, Peter and James and John and Andrew asked him privately, Tell us, when shall these things be? and what shall be the sign when all these things shall be fulfilled? (Mark 13:3-4).

In making a close study of this portion it will be helpful to keep these two questions in mind. They are not identical questions about the same thing. Notice the way they read: "When shall these things be?" I suspect this is a reference to the destruction of the city of Jerusalem. The second question: "What shall be the sign when all these things shall be fulfilled? "All these things" would be the destruction predicted of the whole world.

> And Jesus answering them began to say, Take heed lest any man deceive you: for many shall come in my name, saying, I am Christ; and shall deceive many. And when ye shall hear of wars and rumors of wars, be ye not troubled: for such things must needs be; but the end shall not be yet. For nation shall rise against nation, and kingdom against kingdom: and there shall be earthquakes in divers places, and there shall be famines and troubles: these are the beginnings of sorrows (Mark 13:5-8).

"Take heed lest any man deceive you." For myself I take note that this is one place in the Bible where we can be fooled. This is one place in the whole interpretation of Scripture that begins with a warning: be careful that no one misleads you here. Jesus was saying all this at a time when the Roman Empire extended over the whole known world which was in a condition of what was called "Pax Romana," the peace of Rome, because the whole world was at rest under the control of Rome. There was no apparent reason to expect such chaos.

Calamity and distress will characterize this period in the world. I am inclined to think the period extends from the time Jesus of Nazareth was standing there talking in Jerusalem until the time He returns. This whole period will be marked by this sort of condition. It would seem from history this is still going on, and yet this is only the beginning of sorrows; the end is not yet. There will still be much tribulation (Mark 13:9-23). I would hesitate to take you by the hand and try to lead you through that passage. I do know it says certain things that seem clear enough: e.g., "Take heed to yourselves: for they shall deliver you up to councils; and in the synagogues ye shall be beaten: and ye shall be brought before rulers and kings for my sake, for a testimony against them" (Mark 13:9). There will be persecution of believers and that has been characteristic of this age from the time the Romans persecuted the Christians down to events happening in various parts of the world even today. It seems tragically true in the whole world, they who live godly in Christ Jesus shall suffer persecution, in one way or another.

"And the gospel must first be published among all nations" (Mark 13:10). Many people are keeping in mind that this promise is apparently very definite, and it does seem to imply to a certain extent that the gospel as we understand it must first be published among all nations. This Scripture has in many cases inspired mission work. Two generations ago there was a great movement to evangelize the world in that generation. It was a time when Christians were inspired to undertake the task; many will remember the founding of the organization known as "Christian Endeavor," in which the effort was to be made to get the gospel to the ends of the earth in one generation. There is a similar emphasis today and it now seems to be feasible because of the mass media. By this means the gospel can be spread by radio and television.

We read:

> But when they shall lead you, and deliver you up, take no thought beforehand what ye shall speak, neither do ye premeditate: but whatsoever shall be given you in that hour, that speak ye: for it is not ye that speak, but the Holy Ghost. Now the brother shall betray the brother to death, and the father the son; and children shall rise up against their parents, and shall cause them to be put to death. And ye shall be hated of all men for my name's sake: but he that shall endure unto the end, the same shall be saved (Mark 13:11-13).

In all parts of the world where the gospel is being taught this is the way it happens, even right amongst ourselves.

At a time of great natural catastrophe the Lord will return:

"And then shall they see the Son of man coming in the clouds with great power and glory" (Mark 13:26). Toward the end of the chapter we notice several other points: the return of the Lord is absolutely sure. He really is coming back. In the book of Acts we are told: "This same Jesus . . . shall so come in like manner as ye have seen him go into heaven" (Acts 1:11). The return of the Lord is absolutely sure according to what the Bible teaches. There is another word to keep in mind: the time of His return is unknown. It is not for us to know the times or the season.

This passage concludes with a clear warning: "And what I say unto you I say unto all, Watch" (Mark 13:37). We know not the day or the hour. Watch. Take heed. Watch and pray, for we know not when the time is.

Chapter 46

ANOINTING BY MARY

(Mark 14:1-9)

In our study of Mark's Gospel we have now come to the last few days of the earthly ministry of Jesus of Nazareth. This chapter will focus on one of the sweetest incidents in the entire account of His earthly career. Who would you say is the most widely known woman in the world? Some people will point out that probably it is Mary of Bethany because the Lord has said about her that wherever the gospel is preached the story of Mary's anointing of Jesus of Nazareth should be told.

> After two days was the feast of the passover, and of unleavened bread: and the chief priests and the scribes sought how they might take him by craft, and put him to death. But they said, Not on the feast day, lest there be an uproar of the people. And being in Bethany in the house of Simon the leper, as he sat at meat, there came a woman having an alabaster box of ointment of spikenard very precious; and she brake the box, and poured it on his head. And there were some that had indignation within themselves, and said, Why was this waste of the ointment made? For it might have been sold for more than three hundred pence, and have been given to the poor. And they murmured against her. And Jesus said, Let her alone; why trouble ye her? she hath wrought a good work on me. For ye have the poor with you always, and whensoever ye will ye may do them good: but me ye have not always. She hath done what she could: she is come aforehand to anoint my body to the burying. Verily I say unto you, Wheresoever this gospel shall be preached throughout the whole world, this also that she hath done shall be spoken of for a memorial of her (Mark 14:1-9).

This incident is reported in several of the Gospels and always there is the record of much comment. Let us note three important aspects: first, I want to draw your attention to the act, then I want to speak of the way in which this woman was esteemed by others, and finally I want to raise the question, "What was the woman's secret?"

The act was a simple one: she brought the best she had to

Jesus of Nazareth, personally, as a gift. And that is the whole story. It was the custom when dead bodies were put away in the caves to anoint them, to embalm them with spices to counteract the odor of the decaying flesh. The bodies were then wrapped in linen clothes, such as those used to put mummies away. Mary of Bethany had in mind Jesus was going to die. He was going to die for her, and she came to anoint His body beforehand. This will forever be the basic principle in all blessed giving; namely, turn over the very best I have for Him personally, as a gift.

Mary of Bethany was criticized first of all by the disciples. Criticism is to be expected any time one serves the Lord. The interesting thing here is the criticism does not come from the outside world, but from among believers on the basis that she had done too much. People who do not do much are frequently ready to criticize people who do more. No doubt this is an old custom with human beings: they are always prone to compare self with others. We want to look good in comparison with others. If the other person is far ahead and we do not feel like trying to catch up, there is one thing we can do: pull the other one back, then we won't be too far behind. This is an old human story, and it happens over and over. People do not like to see anyone get ahead of them; so they criticize. This truth is seen in many places, and especially in connection with the Lord's work.

In church work it is a common experience. For example, the church leaders had been looking for someone to lead a certain program, and not being able to find anyone else, they finally came to one young woman. Far more often than is realized, she was the last resort. When they asked her to take the responsibility they made it look as natural as possible, saying, "You are the only person who can do this." If the young woman being asked to do it. protests that she has not had experience, they will tell her there are people around who will help who have done it before. They offer to give her a committee. So the young woman takes the responsibility and when the time comes for the program to be prepared one of the committee members is sick, another has gone to Florida, and so the young woman is alone. She still has to give the program. Now if it happens to be a good one, there will be those who ask, "Why did she do it all by herself? Doesn't she think anyone else can do anything?" She will hear all kinds of criticism from various sources. No doubt many people get discouraged and quit doing the Lord's work for just this very reason: the unfair criticism by others who did nothing.

But on the other hand Mary of Bethany was rated not only

by the disciples but she was rated by the Lord. When they criticized her for what she was doing, saying it was overdone, He told them to let her alone; she had done what she could. The day will come when we will be in the presence of God. None of us will feel very proud and none of us will feel we have accomplished much. Would it not be wonderful when that time comes, knowing all the criticism that could be properly levelled at me, if I could hear the words of the Lord: "Let him alone. He has done what he could and I understand about it." That would be a wonderful experience for me to have!!

And now let us look for a moment to the secret of Mary of Bethany. Why did she do this? How did she know her act would attract such attention from Jesus of Nazareth that He would say this should be told wherever the gospel was preached? Actually, there is no evidence she was conscious of the significance of her act. She did not do what she did because she knew He would say it should be told everywhere. Her reason was much more simple: she loved Him. And why did she love Him in this special way? This is the Mary who sat at Jesus' feet and heard His words. This is the Mary who listened when He spoke. And she loved Him because He first loved her. She knew He loved her and she knew He would give His life for her, and the woman brought the very best she had to Him personally as a gift, regardless of what other people would say, because she loved Him. This is the classic example of serving the Lord.

Chapter 47

JUDAS PLANS TO BETRAY HIM

(Mark 14:10-11)

Judas Iscariot remains one of the great enigmas of history. He is notorious wherever the gospel is preached, and always the question is raised: how could he do it? For more than three years he had been in close fellowship with Jesus of Nazareth, and he had been among those chosen to be His special representatives. Not only was he a disciple among all the disciples, but he was chosen as one of the twelve apostles. There is no detailed account of this falling away in Judas Iscariot but some phases of what he did are recorded. He was one of the twelve disciples who were chosen to represent the gospel to Israel, and he was called an apostle. We have no intimation that during those three years his conduct as a disciple was suspected by anyone as being inferior. John's comment that he was a thief does not refer to outward appearance or deed.

I could raise the question here: who is a thief? Someone may say a thief is a man who steals. I will then ask why did he steal? and before he stole what was he? If you tell me he was an honest man I will tell you an honest man would not steal. You see, the very fact that he stole means he was a thief before he stole. His stealing demonstrated – outwardly showed – he was a thief. Now we come back to this – what was he before he stole? And again, if you say he was an honest man I will tell you an honest man would not steal. When John said he was a thief, he was commenting on his inward attitude.

"And supper being ended, the devil having now put into the heart of Judas Iscariot, Simon's son, to betray him" (John 13:2). That seems to have been the origin of the idea. There is no indication that during the three years he served as an apostle, Judas had in mind he would betray the Lord. "And after the sop Satan entered into him" (John 13:27). Apparently this was a new experience. "Then said Jesus unto him, That thou doest, do quickly." And we read he negotiated with the chief priests to betray Jesus. "And Judas Iscariot, one of the twelve, went unto the chief priests, to betray him unto them. And when they heard it, they were glad, and promised to give him money. And he sought how he might conveniently betray him" (Mark 14:10-11). This is all Mark has to say about the whole story.

Some imaginative and enterprising commentators have proposed that Judas Iscariot had some rational grounds for his action: he was expecting certain things from Jesus of Nazareth that were not forthcoming. But that is not in the story in any of the gospel records. What was his reason? Personally I am inclined toward the idea he was greedy. As I have pointed out before, John tells us he was a thief; and that means he had an inordinate love of money. Everyone appreciates money. We all wish we had more, but it is when I want money first, above all else, that I am foolish in my attitude.

This sad story has a sober warning for all of us. Have you ever thought of this: one can hold a dime so close to his eyes that he cannot see the sun? Many of us may feel virtuous and tell ourselves we wouldn't betray Him for thirty dollars. Can you feel what I am seeking to point out? This man, Judas Iscariot, was one of the disciples of Jesus of Nazareth; more than that, he was one of the apostles. When they were sent out two by two, Judas went with them. He went as one of them. The fact is, Judas Iscariot was a trusted man.

While we are thinking about this, do you remember the occasion when the Lord Jesus at the last supper came to His disciples sadly, and said "One of you shall betray me." Not one person there suspected Judas Iscariot. Each said, "Is it I?" Apparently those disciples did not have the disposition to suspect anyone else. As a matter of fact, when He told them one of the twelve was a weak link in the chain, each man wondered if he was the one. Judas was a man who shared with the other disciples and had done so for three years; a man who had fellowship with Jesus Christ: and yet he could actually be snared by this very thing, because he loved money. Money is something selfish; and any time you catch me in anything wherein I am looking out for myself, I am walking right alongside Judas Iscariot.

Think about this: when a person would rather go to some social affair instead of going to a church service, what are you going to say about him? Or how about a person who spends a large sum of money for tickets to sports events and does not give anything to missions? Would you recognize anything in that? Is that person really the same type of person Judas Iscariot was? How about a person who is more interested in the personal friendship of other people than he is in giving his testimony for the Lord? Or the person who knows when something is not right but won't say anything about it because he may get in wrong with someone. Do you recognize this was the same spirit Judas Iscariot had?

When I bring these matters up I am telling myself that even those who walk with the Lord should walk in fear and trembling (1 Peter 1:17) lest in some odd moment, in some unexpected way, they suddenly find themselves right where they are doing the very thing this man did. Will you understand me if I say he really did not want to do this? How do I know? Because when he realized what he had done, he went out and hanged himself. To betray his Lord was not really his mind, if we want to word it that way. It was not the kind of thing he would characteristically do; but he fell into it, and believe me, he fell all the way down.

The Scripture says that he "went to his own place." There is no attempt to gloss over that. This action on his part is recognized in the Bible, and throughout the world, as the outstanding act of betrayal. We do not know what Judas had in mind when he did this, but we do know that when he came to himself he went out and hanged himself. This is a sober line of thought. We can only humbly turn to the Lord and say, "O God, keep us from falling into such a snare."

Chapter 48

PREPARATION FOR THE PASSOVER FEAST

(Mark 14:12-16)

As the days pass we come to days in the course of every year that are special. We have Christmas, Easter and Thanksgiving. In our own families there are anniversaries, and in our communities there are annual events of various sorts. In our families we celebrate birthdays, graduations and weddings. I think this is good. The human being does well to pay special attention to important events. In the culture of Israel there were stated feasts, and certain times in the year when they fasted. They had also holy days and certain special sabbaths. Observing these events helped to keep certain facts in mind and heart.

In our own culture we have special observances, and this is a healthy thing. When we celebrate Christmas, it is true there may be many human elements in it that are not desirable, but the idea of remembering the coming of the Lord is helpful. We are blessed when we have our families together every day all year long, but there is no harm in celebrating the anniversary of your wedding day even though it happened long ago.

> And the first day of unleavened bread, when they killed the passover, his disciples said unto him, Where wilt thou that we go and prepare that thou mayest eat the passover? And he sendeth forth two of his disciples, and saith unto them, Go ye into the city, and there shall meet you a man bearing a pitcher of water: follow him. And wheresoever he shall go in, say ye to the goodman of the house, The Master saith, Where is the guest chamber, where I shall eat the passover with my disciples? And he will show you a large upper room furnished and prepared: there make ready for us. And his disciples went forth, and came into the city, and found as he had said unto them: and they made ready the passover (Mark 14:12-16).

We are given no clue in this story as to how those practical details were arranged or even if they were arranged. How did the Lord know a man would be walking on the street with a pitcher of water, and that he would lead the apostles to an upper room already furnished for them? Had there been some arrangement made beforehand? We do not know. I hope no one feels impatient that I raise this question. I know it is a practical thing, but I want to move on from there and take note of some other aspects of the story: the disciples took no initiative before He told them. He told them what to do and they went out to do what He said. The Lord guided them in what they were to do and they were obedient to Him. The upper room was already furnished and everything was fully prepared. They were going to observe the passover there. This was a special worship situation. We can also notice that when all had been prepared, others were willing to share.

These are principles we do well to keep in mind. As we reflect on this whole matter we will remember that sometimes in our own congregations, when we are having the sacrament of the Lord's Supper, there are preparatory services when people take time to prepare themselves to come to the table of the Lord. How would one prepare in this fashion? Let us remember there is such a thing as preparing to have fellowship with Him. There is such a thing as preparing to worship Him.

Consider the ministry of John the Baptist, who came to prepare the way of the King: to open the doors, as it were, for Him. John did this by preaching repentance. This is an order of events we should follow: repent, confess your sins, believe on the Lord, and receive from God. That is the sequence of what happens in the will of God. How will we do that ordinarily? First we come into the presence of God feeling our unfitness, we are not worthy of Him. I can say for myself that if I do not feel I am not worthy of God, then I do not have Him in mind. There need be no difficulty about meeting the first requirement. We are not to make any excuse for the way we have conducted ourselves; we do not come into God's presence to offer an alibi as to our conduct. We do not try to explain away our guilt, we humbly confess that we are unworthy. We may come as did Isaiah:

> Woe is me! for I am undone; because I am a man of unclean lips, and I dwell in the midst of a people of unclean lips: for mine eyes have seen the King, the Lord of hosts (Isa. 6:5).

Isaiah felt his own unfitness, partly because of the very people with whom he lived. That is admitting the situation as it is. Or we may recognize our condition as Job who said:

> I have heard of thee by the hearing of the ear; but now mine eye seeth thee: wherefore I abhor myself, and repent in dust and ashes (Job 42:5-6).

This attitude is the beginning. This happens when we open our hearts to God, turn to God and face Him. This is basic.

After this we confess our sins. Actually while we are kneeling there before God, looking up into His face, it is never long until there comes to mind something that hasn't been right: something that we have done or should not have done: something we failed to do that we should have done. And so we turn to God.

Repenting and confessing is like emptying out what is wrong. Now, in the presence of God, we are to believe His promises. He has promised that if we come unto Him and trust and believe in Him, we will be forgiven. We will not perish but have everlasting life. If someone says he is not fit, that is true. But that is no longer the issue. He has died for me: I should believe it! He wants me to come to Him: I should believe it! Believing is responding. It is putting my trust in Him! It is committing myself to Him! Now I cling to His promises. He will give me His Holy Spirit to come into my heart when I commit myself to Him. I can always remember one thing with joy, as I prepare myself for fellowship with the Lord: a humble and a contrite heart the Lord will not despise.

Chapter 49

THE LAST SUPPER

(Mark 14:17-31)

We come now to the last events in the earthly career of Jesus of Nazareth. We will be looking at the Last Supper. Not all of the details of that supper are reported but some have been recorded, and we will do well to look at this account again.

> And in the evening he cometh with the twelve. And as they sat and did eat, Jesus said, Verily I say unto you, One of you which eateth with me shall betray me. And they began to be sorrowful, and to say unto him one by one, Is it I? and another said, Is it I? And he answered and said unto them, It is one of the twelve, that dippeth with me in the dish. The Son of man indeed goeth, as it is written of him: but woe to that man by whom the Son of man is betrayed! good were it for that man if he had never been born (Mark 14:17-21).

This carries a simple message: He would be betrayed by one of His own. It is not clear to me why, in the providence of God, it should work out that one of His own should tell the soldiers where He was. What comes to mind is this: I wouldn't have thought the disciples as a whole were so hidden, that their meetings and fellowships together were unknown to the public. One would think that anyone could know where they were; but for some reason it is all set out plainly that it took someone to guide the soldiers to where the disciples were. Among them was this Person, Jesus of Nazareth. The implication is clear, however, and the story is accurate: one of His own disciples helped the soldiers arrest Him. When He had told them this would happen, there is evidence He was deeply affected: "He was troubled in spirit, and testified, and said, Verily, verily, I say unto you, that one of you shall betray me" (John 13:21). Mark simply said: "One of you which eateth with me shall betray me."

No one suspected Judas and I think it is worthy of note that each man had the feeling, if there is anyone who is weak, it is I: each in turn said: "Lord, is it I?" Then the Lord made a comment that to my mind was ominous: "Woe to that man by whom the Son of man is betrayed! good were it for that man if he had never been born."

What do you personally think of Jesus of Nazareth? What is in your mind about Him? Do you share the popular notion that He was the kind of person anyone could mistreat, and it would be all right? Do you have the idea He was a person who took no offense about anything? The above words of His sober us. This is what it amounts to: the way I treat Jesus of Nazareth is known in heaven and judged by God. How easy it is to be preoccupied with other things and leave Him out! He is the Father's beloved Son in whom the Father is well pleased, and the Father is depicted as being vitally concerned about the attention given to Jesus of Nazareth. If I turn my back on the Lord Jesus Christ, He will turn His back on me. If I forget the Lord Jesus Christ I will yet have to say He will never forget me.

> And as they did eat, Jesus took bread, and blessed, and brake it, and gave to them, and said, Take, eat: this is my body. And he took the cup, and when he had given thanks, he gave it to them: and they all drank of it. And he said unto them. This is my blood of the new testament, which is shed for many. Verily I say unto you, I will drink no more of the fruit of the vine, until that day that I drink it new in the kingdom of God (Mark 14:22-25).

Even though Mark gives only the bare details, it is clearly seen that participation is personal: sharing in the things of the Lord Jesus Christ is done by the individual. The eating and drinking is done one by one!

> And Jesus saith unto them, All ye shall be offended because of me this night: for it is written, I will smite the shepherd, and the sheep shall be scattered. But after that I am risen, I will go before you into Galilee. But Peter said unto him, Although all shall be offended, yet will not I. And Jesus saith unto him. Verily I say unto thee, That this day, even in this night, before the cock crow twice, thou shalt deny me thrice. But he spake the more vehemently, If I should die with thee, I will not deny thee in any wise. Likewise also said they all (Mark 14:27-31).

Peter's strong affirmation that he would not deny Him was repeated with emphasis. We should note that all the disciples said it, not just Peter. They all went together in their protestation of loyalty. It is instructive to note Peter's self-confident assertion, and then the Lord's prediction.

These are serious events we are reading about, dealing with Jesus of Nazareth personally; and it seems clear the implications come close to each of us who believe. We need to turn humbly to the Lord and ask Him to be merciful and gracious, and to remember we are just human beings. It is so easy for us to become absorbed with other matters. We ask the Almighty God to forgive us for the times when we have failed to appreciate the things of the Lord Jesus Christ.

Chapter 50

THE GARDEN OF GETHSEMANE

(Mark 14:32-42)

Of all the events recorded in the gospel about the earthly career of Jesus of Nazareth, probably one of the best known is what happened at the Garden of Gethsemane. Each of the Gospels tells about it. It would be helpful to read all four accounts to appreciate what happened.

> And they came to a place which was named Gethsemane: and he saith to his disciples, Sit ye here, while I shall pray. And he taketh with him Peter and James and John, and began to be sore amazed, and to be very heavy; and saith unto them, My soul is exceeding sorrowful unto death; tarry ye here, and watch. And he went forward a little, and fell on the ground, and prayed that, if it were possible, the hour might pass from him. And he said, Abba, Father, all things are possible unto thee; take away this cup from me: nevertheless not what I will, but what thou wilt. And he cometh, and findeth them sleeping, and saith unto Peter, Simon, sleepest thou? couldest not thou watch one hour? Watch ye and pray, lest ye enter into temptation. The spirit truly is ready, but the flesh is weak. And again he went away, and prayed, and spake the same words. And when he returned, he found them asleep again, (for their eyes were heavy,) neither wist they what to answer him. And he cometh the third time, and saith unto them, Sleep on now, and take your rest: it is enough, the hour is come; behold, the Son of man is betrayed into the hands of sinners. Rise up, let us go; lo, he that betrayeth me is at hand (Mark 14:32-42).

Whenever I think about that night in the Garden of Gethsemane, I have a feeling in my heart almost as if I were an intruder. It seems almost impertinent for me to look at this account, yet I realize it was written for me. It was intended by the Holy Spirit that I should read this and by His grace learn certain things revealed here. Look at it closely: "And he saith to his disciples, Sit ye here, while I shall pray." Prayer is to be made by all persons; and to be effective it should be performed by each person. Yet some people pray more than others; and there are those who pray when others do not. "And he taketh with him Peter, and James and John, and began to be sore amazed, and to be very heavy." The impression seems clear that He was now going to pray about something unusually important. He took with Him certain persons. This seems to be an inner circle; not that these disciples were set off from others or limited in the sense no one else could join them; but it means that characteristically not all believers are in the same relationship with the Lord. There can be an inner circle of those who join Him when He goes the extra, the "second mile."

As we think of these three men we might note that Peter is first. There are things we commonly carry in our minds about Peter, and then there are things we commonly forget about him. We are quick to think of him as being impulsive and vulnerable. We remember that when the time came – the test – he even denied his Lord. Seldom do we remember that when the inner circle of those who were close to the Lord Jesus Christ is mentioned, Peter is at the head of the list. Despite his humanity, and in spite of his occasional failure, even so he qualified as one of the inner circle. Frankly, this gives me an inner challenge and encouragement. Just because my record is not perfect and because my actual performance may be rather spotty does not mean I cannot be close to the Lord. I can have fellowship with Him.

There are other surprising points here quite beyond my understanding: "...and began to be sore amazed." This seems to imply He was filled with horror and distress, and He began to "be very heavy." That is an old English idiom to convey the idea He was deeply disturbed and depressed. He was burdened. He had not shown this to the public in general. "And saith unto them, My soul is exceeding sorrowful unto death: tarry ye here, and watch." I raise the question for myself: what could this have meant? What did the Lord Jesus Christ face that was so awful that He was filled with horror? I cannot think this was physical death, for I do not think physical death would have held such terrors for Him. And He knew that on the third day He would be raised from the dead.

There is probably more involved here than I can ever know, and we are looking at something far beyond us. However, I will share with you some thoughts that come to me: there must have been confronting Him some prospect of separation from His Father. This was awful because of the great everlasting love the Father and the Son had for each other. We will never fully appreciate what Jesus Christ did for us until we realize it meant He would be separated from His Father.

He said to them: "Tarry ye here, and watch." This is how we

can have fellowship with His suffering. I want to bear in mind personally this is what He endured for me. He went forward a little and fell on the ground, and prayed that if it were possible the hour might pass from Him. Have you ever had the feeling of shrinking away from some test? If this is the case you should not let it discourage you. This does not mean necessarily there is anything wrong with you. It is not the man without fear who is brave: it is the man who fears, because he knows what is involved, yet carries on in spite of his fear. At this point Jesus of Nazareth made an interesting statement: "If it be possible take away this cup from me, nevertheless not what I will, but what thou wilt." Here we can see the difference between what I would call His request and His prayer. We are told in the Bible to let our requests be made known unto God. If He had been asked in a human way what He would want, He would have said, "I want to miss this experience." That would be His request, but that wasn't His prayer. Here is His prayer: "Nevertheless not what I will, but what thou wilt."

We know the remainder of that story; how, when He came He found these chosen men sleeping. We should not be too harsh on those disciples. It was late at night, probably some time about midnight. He had been praying for one hour. Have you ever been at a prayer meeting where they prayed for as long as one hour in continuous praying? If that has been the case and you should have been sleepy or fallen asleep, I hope you would not feel too distressed. You are just a human being. In the next sentence the Lord Jesus said: "Watch ye and pray, lest ye enter into temptation. The spirit truly is ready, but the flesh is weak." He came three times and that means He must have spent about three hours in prayer. He then said: "Sleep on now, and take your rest: it is enough, the hour is come."

This is indeed a hallowed spot in the record in the gospel of the Lord Jesus Christ, when Jesus of Nazareth Himself faced the prospect of being separated from His Father. In other passages of Scripture we get the impression the experience could have killed Him if He had not been strengthened by an angel. I should privately remember this was on my account.

Chapter 51

JESUS OF NAZARETH ARRESTED BY SOLDIERS

(Mark 14:43-52)

In the wisdom of God there are times when the natural opposition to the things of Jesus Christ come in like a flood, and it would seem all that matters is being swept away. Apparently God allows such times of testing to come to His people, when it seems as though everything one had confidence in is being shaken. There are also times when things seem to be coming our way in the full tide of victory. Jacob had the experience of feeling that everything was going wrong for him:

> Me have ye bereaved of my children: Joseph is not, and Simeon is not, and ye will take Benjamin away: all these things are against me (Gen. 42:36).

How often we have felt like that! Not only do such times come, but God permits this to happen. It is common experience to say "nothing succeeds like success," and even so, defeats lead into depression.

One of the outstanding aspects of the earthly career of the Son of God came when He seemed to lose all: when everything seemed to be against Him.

> And immediately, while he yet spake, cometh Judas, one of the twelve, and with him a great multitude with swords and staves, from the chief priests and the scribes and the elders. And he that betrayed him had given them a token, saying, Whomsoever I shall kiss, that same is he; take him, and lead him away safely. And as soon as he was come, he goeth straightway to him, and saith, Master, master; and kissed him. And they laid their hands on him, and took him (Mark 14:43-46).

As usual Mark records the facts in stark reality; he makes no comments. He simply tells what happened. Judas had planned well how to betray the Lord, and he accomplished it successfully. The soldiers took Him away. In Matthew, Luke and John there are more details.

> And Jesus answered and said unto them, Are ye come out,

> as against a thief, with swords and with staves to take me? I was daily with you in the temple teaching, and ye took me not: but the scriptures must be fulfilled. And they all forsook him, and fled. And there followed him a certain young man, having a linen cloth cast about his naked body; and the young men laid hold on him: and he left the linen cloth, and fled from them naked (Mark 14:48-52).

Although Jesus of Nazareth showed He understood the evil in their actions, and knew what they were doing, yet He yielded to them: for, "the Scriptures must be fulfilled." He was to be falsely accused and improperly condemned. He was to be taken by wicked hands and eventually slain.

Mark does not name Peter in this account though others do. Peter was going to defend Jesus of Nazareth and he demonstrated the unwise, natural reaction of a loyal supporter, but not the spiritual reaction. A sincere follower feels like fighting, and in loyalty Peter was ready to do so. The truth is, however, that in obedience he should yield: he should lose in order to win. "And they all forsook him, and fled." It is one thing to profess, and to make public claims, but it is quite another to stay faithful and to yield and to lose because that is what the Lord wants the believer to do. This is the way it was with the disciples.

There has been speculation on the part of some scholars as to who the young man who ran away was. The Bible doesn't tell us. There is no clue, and we would be wise just to leave it at that. It is worthy of noting that all those who belonged to Him ran. We should not blame them. They were face to face with a cruel mob and their leader, Jesus of Nazareth Himself, had yielded. There was nothing left for them to do but to get out.

This whole incident brings to our attention an unhappy thought: at a time when public esteem hardens into dislike and rejection, it is natural for lesser souls to withdraw. It is not hard to see why believers withdraw when there is opposition. But we are reminded now that it was Jesus of Nazareth, the Son of God, the King of Kings, the Lord of all, who was in this situation. He was betrayed by a follower, and taken by wicked hands. He was manhandled by unbelieving people, and He did not resist. All believers will feel the challenge of this event. It is hard to accept, but there is no indication this means Jesus of Nazareth was weak. We need to ask ourselves: which takes more strength — to fight or to yield? Which takes more confidence: to contend and quarrel, or to yield and allow wrong to prevail? How easy it is for people to get worked up and think if a thing is right, we should fight for it. If a thing is wrong we should fight against it: if the word is "fight" we should fight all the way through. But the will of God may be not to "fight" but to "yield."

Jesus told Pilate: "My kingdom is not of this world: if my kingdom were of this world, then would my servants fight" (John 18:36). But the Lord and His disciples did not fight, because His kingdom was not of this world. And because His kingdom is not of this world, it means this world can actually witness evil in strong power triumphing. On the contrary, those who are against God may seem to have the victory, but it will be only for a time. We would be wise to remember this and to watch our own fervor; we need to be careful about these matters.

When those who are against the Lord seem to triumph, and the people who make fun of Him and the gospel seem to have everything going their way, the effect on people generally dulls the heart. On one occasion the Lord Himself, in predicting these times, said: "Because iniquity shall abound, the love of many shall wax cold" (Matt. 24:12). It may happen that way but it would be a mistake to think this is the end. We need to learn how to strengthen our faith and how to encourage our own devotion, to make sure we are strong in our testimony. Sometimes things go against us in a big way, in a way altogether unreasonable, and the forces of evil and darkness may seem to prevail. It is for you and for me to keep in mind the Lord Himself sits on the throne, and the enemy can only go so far. God has marked the limits beyond which they cannot go.

The One who sits in heaven marks the boundaries of the sea and no matter how the waves of the ocean may roll toward the shore, they can only go so far. Their distance, their reach, is determined by Almighty God. And so it is with the actions of men. Although evil may seem to prosper, you and I are to remember the Lord is God and He will prevail. This is what needs to be thought about when we notice these times in the life of Jesus of Nazareth. Everything was against Him even if He was God. Everything else seeming to rule: and He was almighty. Everything else seemed to belittle Him: but He was the King of Kings and the Lord of all. It is for believers to look at Him and believe this, and rejoice in it; for His name's sake they can do this.

Chapter 52

ON TRIAL BEFORE THE HIGH PRIEST

(Mark 14:53-65)

The death of Jesus of Nazareth at the hands of the Roman soldiers by crucifixion is an item of history, conceded by everyone as a notorious fact. What may not always be realized is that this tragic event was brought about by the malicious hostility of the priests and the outcry of the mob on the street. The Roman Governor, Pontius Pilate, had personally no cause for persecution, no animosity against Jesus of Nazareth as a person; but the rulers of the Jews wanted Him to be put to death. They were not free to do this themselves. Rome was in political control of the country, and because their government had authority over the Jewish councils and court, their rules were the ones that had to be followed. They permitted individual groups in their empire to have their own local laws, and so they permitted the Jews to have their own laws and their own courts for Jewish affairs. They could try Jesus of Nazareth in court for breaking the law of the Jews, and if their sentence was execution they could petition the Roman Governor to perform this execution: and this is what they did.

The first trial of Jesus of Nazareth was staged before the Jewish court, before the High Priest. Here He was charged with blasphemy, because that was a capital crime with the Jews. But no man would be put to death in the Roman Empire because he blasphemed against a certain god; whereas with the Jewish people any one of them who blasphemed against God was subject to death. Later they would go before Pontius Pilate and there Jesus of Nazareth would be accused of treason, which was subject to death in the Roman court. Just now as Jesus of Nazareth is standing before the Jewish court He is accused of blasphemy. If He had been accused of treason before the Jewish court He could not have been condemned to death because this was not in their law, and the Jews were not in favor of the Romans anyway.

And the chief priests and all the council sought for witness

> against Jesus to put him to death; and found none (Mark 14:55).

They searched for someone to accuse Him of some crime worthy of death and they could not find a thing with which they could accuse Him. "For many bare false witness against him, but their witness agreed not together" (Mark 14:56). When some witness said He had done something wrong, actual cross examination would bring out the fact that no one would support the accusation. Evidently the court was following some semblance of justice; they tried to work things out to get a clear indictment against Jesus of Nazareth from those who knew Him.

> And there arose certain, and bare false witness against him, saying, We heard him say, I will destroy this temple that is made with hands, and within three days I will build another made without hands. But neither so did their witness agree together (Mark 14:57-59).

When we compare the record of John with others as to what Jesus of Nazareth said about this, we notice a little difference. He did say, "If you destroy this temple, I will restore it"; but this was not so much to destroy this temple building which is made with hands. He was not referring to that stone temple, He was referring to the temple of His body, as we read in John's Gospel. The point is, when they brought this accusation against Him, saying He made claims that were unfounded and untrue, no one would agree even then as to what there was against Him.

> And the high priest stood up in the midst, and asked Jesus, saying, Answerest thou nothing? what is it which these witness against thee? But he held his peace, and answered nothing (Mark 14:60-61).

This is one of those rare moments that we get a glimpse of what actually took place. While these people were accusing Him falsely, He did not say a word: He just let their accusation stand. In many cases the accusation they offered fell to the ground unsupported.

> Again the high priest asked him, and said unto him, Art thou the Christ, the Son of the Blessed? And Jesus said, I am: and ye shall see the Son of man sitting on the right hand of power, and coming in the clouds of heaven. Then the high priest rent his clothes, and saith, What need we any further witnesses? Ye have heard the blasphemy: what think ye? And they all condemned him to be guilty of death (Mark 14:61-64).

When they could not bring anything else against Him their reaction was one of fury! It threw all of them into an uproar, and they condemned Him to be guilty of death. These were the public leaders of religion, and before we let this pass unnoticed, what do you think? When have you heard this truth soberly announced from your pulpit? Have you ever heard your preacher say you would see the Son of Man sitting on the right hand of power and coming in the clouds of heaven? Some of you have and you are fortunate, but I have been in many churches to hear men preach when I listened for this and could not get even a glimmer that they had the idea the time would come when the Son of Man would be sitting on the right hand of power and coming in the clouds of heaven.

> And some began to spit on him, and to cover his face, and to buffet him, and to say unto him, Prophesy: and the servants did strike him with the palms of their hands (Mark 14:65).

Some of the other Gospels are more specific. They report that when they hit Him they covered His face and then asked Him, "Who hit you? If you know everything, tell us about that." The vulgar mob abused Him. What gave them that sense of liberty? When the leaders were seen rejecting Him, it is no surprise the common people were then carried to great lengths in their rejection of Him.

Have you ever wondered why anyone today would ridicule Jesus of Nazareth? They do. If you live in a quiet community and have never seen anything happen but such as transpires around the church among people who are professing believers, you won't know what I am talking about. But if you have been in the big cities and in the universities of our land you know there are men and women who, without any fear of consequence whatever, make fun of and actually lampoon and ridicule the Word of Scripture about Jesus Christ. We have all been shocked by some of the crude things done today against the name of the Lord Jesus Christ by those who do not know any better. When the leaders reject any aspect of the gospel the people will despise that very thing.

Chapter 53

THE DENIAL BY PETER

(Mark 14:66-72)

The denial by Peter is the almost unbelievable incident known to everyone who has heard the gospel story. What is often overlooked is that Peter himself was actually ensnared by his own foolishness to do something he did not really want to do.

> And as Peter was beneath in the palace, there cometh one of the maids of the high priest: and when she saw Peter warming himself, she looked upon him, and said, And thou also wast with Jesus of Nazareth. But he denied, saying, I know not, neither understand I what thou sayest. And he went out into the porch; and the cock crew. And a maid saw him again, and began to say to them that stood by, This is one of them. And he denied it again. And a little after, they that stood by said again to Peter, Surely thou art one of them: for thou art a Galilean, and thy speech agreeth thereto. But he began to curse and to swear, saying, I know not this man of whom ye speak. And the second time the cock crew. And Peter called to mind the word that Jesus said unto him, Before the cock crow twice, thou shalt deny me thrice. And when he thought thereon, he wept (Mark 14:66-72).

This whole tragic story should always be told from the beginning; no one should read only part of it. The reader should remember what is recorded earlier:

> And he (speaking of the Lord Jesus) spake that saying openly. And Peter took him, and began to rebuke him. But when he had turned about and looked on his disciples, he rebuked Peter, saying, Get thee behind me, Satan: for thou savorest not the things that be of God, but the things that be of men (Mark 8:32-33).

The word "savor" has the same meaning as "taste." Jesus of Nazareth was saying in effect, "You don't taste like God, you taste like a man. Your thoughts are not the thoughts of God, you have the thoughts of men." This indicates that when Jesus of Nazareth predicted His rejection, death and resurrection Peter was thinking like a man. Later Jesus of Nazareth said unto them:

> All ye shall be offended because of me this night: for it is written, I will smite the shepherd, and the sheep shall be scattered. But after that I am risen, I will go before you into Galilee. But Peter said unto him, Although all shall be offended, yet will not I (Mark 14:27-29).

Here the record shows Peter self-confident, absolutely sure he would never deny his Lord.

> And he taketh with him Peter and James and John, and began to be sore amazed, and to be very heavy; and saith unto them, My soul is exceeding sorrowful unto death: tarry ye here, and watch. And he went forward a little, and fell on the ground, and prayed that, if it were possible, the hour might pass from him. And he said, Abba, Father, all things are possible unto thee; take away this cup from me: nevertheless not what I will, but what thou wilt. And he cometh, and findeth them sleeping, and saith unto Peter, Simon, sleepest thou? couldest not thou watch one hour? Watch ye and pray, lest ye enter into temptation. The spirit truly is ready, but the flesh is weak (Mark 14:33-38).

When Jesus of Nazareth entered Gethsemane to pray, Peter was sleeping when he could have been praying. This is what is to be seen about Peter thus far: he was thinking like a man and therefore self-confident; now, when his Lord goes to pray, Peter falls asleep. Then we read about the soldiers:

> And they laid their hands on him, and took him. And one of them that stood by drew a sword, and smote a servant of the high priest, and cut off his ear (Mark 14:46-47).

Mark does not tell us that this was Peter, but the other Gospels tell us it was Peter who resisted the Roman soldiers. Here we see that when Jesus of Nazareth yielded to this cruel arrest by the Roman soldiers, Peter was fighting instead of yielding. Put all this together and an important truth can be seen: the man who is sleeping when he could be praying is oftentimes the man who will be fighting instead of yielding.

> And they led Jesus away to the high priest: and with him were assembled all the chief priests and the elders and the scribes. And Peter followed him afar off (Mark 14:53-54).

It should be recognized that Peter followed, and we should not dismiss him as unworthy altogether; however, he followed afar off. And now we will learn that this was the source of his trouble: he followed *afar off*. The sordid record shows that Jesus of Nazareth had already been condemned to death and abused by the mob.

> And some began to spit on him, and to cover his face, and to buffet him, and to say unto him, Prophesy: and the servants did strike him with the palms of their hands. And

> as Peter was beneath in the palace, there cometh one of the maids of the high priest: and when she saw Peter warming himself . . . (Mark 14:65-67).

This happened in the early hours of the morning in an outdoors courtyard when Peter was warming himself at the fire of these unbelieving people, who were really his enemies. Thus he was unconsciously leaving himself open to this big blunder.

> But he denied, saying, I know not, neither understand I what thou sayest. And he went out into the porch; and the cock crew. And a maid saw him again, and began to say to them that stood by, This is one of them. And he denied it again. And a little after, they that stood by said again to Peter, Surely thou art one of them: for thou art a Galilean, and thy speech agreeth thereto (Mark 14:68-70).

While Peter was standing there he wasn't keeping quiet. He was doing what many people do: talking a lot to cover up his mistake. And when they said they could tell by his manner of speech he was a Galilean, he denied Jesus again. So when Jesus of Nazareth was being rejected in the court of the High Priest, Peter denied he ever knew the Lord.

Let us review what we have before us about Peter. It began in this manner: thinking like a man, Peter was confident he would never deny the Lord; sleeping when he should have been praying; fighting when he should have been yielding; following afar off; warming himself at the fire of his enemy. He was actually ready to make a big blunder and he did. He denied he ever knew the Lord and the rooster crowed again. Peter called to mind the word of Jesus: "Before the cock crow twice, thou shalt deny me thrice. And when he thought thereon, he wept." Others tell us he wept bitterly. But the story of Peter should not end here, because it does not end here in the Bible. When Jesus of Nazareth was risen from the dead the angel told Mary Magdalene, "Tell his disciples and Peter that he goeth before you into Galilee" (Mark 16:7). A special message from Jesus to Peter just six weeks later was "Follow thou me" (John 21:22).

It was Peter who did the preaching at Pentecost when 3,000 people were turned to the Lord. This is the same man. What happened? On the Day of Pentecost the Holy Spirit came and filled them; and when the Holy Spirit was in him, Peter was able to speak out. When he stood before the Jewish court he boldly said to them:

> Neither is there salvation in any other: for there is none other name under heaven given among men, whereby we must be saved (Acts 4:12).

The people in the court were amazed that this unlearned man

could speak out so boldly. But they understood when "they took knowledge of them, that they had been with Jesus." This meant they had seen the Lord after His resurrection and were talking from personal experience.

The Jewish leaders had seen Peter beaten and then rejoice in the Lord.

> And they departed from the presence of the council, rejoicing that they were counted worthy to suffer shame for his name (Acts 5:41).

This was the same man who shrank because a girl made fun of him when he was challenged in front of the pagan soldiers and yet a short time later after being beaten he went out from the presence of the council rejoicing he was counted worthy to suffer shame for His name. It is wonderful to know that no matter how weak we may be in ourselves, by the grace of God we can actually be strong in the Lord to the glory of His name.

Chapter 54

THE TRIAL BEFORE PILATE

(Mark 15:1-15)

All the world knows that Jesus of Nazareth was condemned to death in the court of the Roman Governor, Pontius Pilate.

> And straightway in the morning the chief priests held a consultation with the elders and scribes and the whole council, and bound Jesus, and carried him away, and delivered him to Pilate (Mark 15:1).

The trial in the high priest's court had been held during the night. Jesus of Nazareth had gone to the Garden of Gethsemane with His disciples and had taken Peter, James and John with Him into the inner part. He had spent several hours in prayer. It was while He was returning from Gethsemane that the soldiers, led by Judas Iscariot, arrested Jesus of Nazareth. It was probably about midnight when the trial by the high priest was held. The next day was for them the Sabbath, and the court could not have been held on the Sabbath day. When they had condemned Him they held a consultation about the action they should now take. After this they bound Jesus and brought Him before the Roman Governor.

The fact that the next day was the Sabbath did not mean anything to the Roman Governor, so the Roman court would be held. Jesus was accused there of treason, because His condemnation for blasphemy meant nothing to the Romans.

> And Pilate asked him, Art thou the King of the Jews? And he answering said unto him, Thou sayest it. And the chief priests accused him of many things: but he answered nothing (Mark 15:2-3).

Apparently there were trumped-up charges to make Him appear a disorderly person or a criminal, but His accusers were unable to prove anything. In the course of all that was going on, Jesus of Nazareth answered nothing.

> And Pilate asked him again, saying, Answerest thou nothing? behold how many things they witness against thee.

> But Jesus yet answered nothing; so that Pilate marveled (Mark 15:4-5).

It seemed incredible to Pilate that this man would put up no defense, especially since some of the things of which they accused Him were obviously not true, because they were not substantiated by witnesses. This being the case Pilate thought Jesus of Nazareth would have answered, but He did not. Other reports record some of the conversation between Pilate and Jesus of Nazareth in which, when Pilate asked if He was the King, He said, "Yes, but my kingdom is not of this world." And He told Pilate that if His Kingdom had been of this world His servants would be fighting, but since His Kingdom was not of this world, they would not be fighting. The result was the same. Mark simply says Jesus answered nothing.

Apparently Pilate was hoping he could get out of the responsibility of condemning this man. "Now at that feast he released unto them one prisoner, whomsoever they desired" (Mark 15:6). This was the custom of the Romans, who did this to ingratiate themselves with the people they were governing. The Roman government was a foreign power in control of Judea and the Jewish people resented their control. To placate the people the Romans showed every now and again some consideration for them.

> And there was one named Barabbas, which lay bound with them that had made insurrection with him, who had committed murder in the insurrection (Mark 15:7).

Evidently this Barabbas was the leader of an underworld group of bandits, and they had rebelled against the government. In the course of their insurrection a man had been killed and Barabbas was in prison along with his gang.

> And the multitude crying aloud began to desire him to do as he had ever done unto them. But Pilate answered them, saying, Will ye that I release unto you the King of the Jews? For he knew that the chief priests had delivered him for envy (Mark 15:8-10).

The multitude wanted Pilate to release a prisoner. It would have pleased Pilate to have released Jesus of Nazareth because he did not want to condemn Him. However this may strike your own heart and mind, if you want to have any sympathy for Pilate you could have it at this point. Apparently he did not personally think anything was wrong with Jesus of Nazareth.

> But the chief priests moved the people, that he should rather release Barabbas unto them. And Pilate answered and said again unto them, What will ye then that I shall do

> unto him whom ye call the King of the Jews? And they cried out again, Crucify him (Mark 15:11-13).

In different parts of the world and in different cultures various methods have been used to put a person to death; crucifixion was the Roman way of putting a person to death.

> Then Pilate said unto them, Why, what evil hath he done? And they cried out the more exceedingly, Crucify him. And so Pilate, willing to content the people, released Barabbas unto them, and delivered Jesus, when he had scourged him, to be crucified (Mark 15:14-15).

In this whole sad story it seems the outstanding thing was the foolishness of this man, Pontius Pilate. In many ways he resembled a modern, successful businessman. He was governor of that part of the country, a position of prominence. This action was not something in which he wanted to be involved. He had no personal animus against Jesus of Nazareth, and personally he felt He was innocent. Pilate was in a position of authority where he could have released Him. He offered them a murderer and naturally thought the people would choose the good man but he was fooled in that. They insisted on putting Jesus to death, and Pilate consented. What makes it so obnoxious to us is that he knew better, but he consented because he thought it would be to his advantage.

We cannot help but feel that Pilate apparently had good sentiments. If left to his own choice he would not have done this, but under the pressure of public opinion he allowed himself to be swayed. It is hard to dwell upon Pilate, because he resembles so many modern businessmen who have personal ambition. They want to get along in the world. They want to have a certain group of friends, and to accomplish this they cannot afford to be involved in anything that would be of a religious nature. So they turn away from the things of God and the gospel, and give themselves over to things that are worldly and selfish; they think these may serve their own interests. This is just plain foolishness.

Can you ever recall knowing anyone who was named Pilate? People do not want to give that name to a child. Yet Pilate in himself was a good man, one who had sentiments and feelings probably quite decent; but he did this wrong to political advantage.

Chapter 55

THE CRUCIFIXION

(Mark 15:16-37)

The story of the crucifixion of Jesus of Nazareth is an ugly story of man's inhumanity to man. It pictures in simple, stark terms the distressing cruelty endured by the Son of God. When we read about this we will be walking, as it were, soberly in the presence of these events. After Jesus of Nazareth had been condemned He was scourged, and then turned over to the soldiers to be crucified.

> And the soldiers led him away into the hall, called Pretorium; and they call together the whole band. And they clothed him with purple, and plaited a crown of thorns, and put it about his head, and began to salute him, Hail, King of the Jews! And they smote him on the head with a reed, and did spit upon him, and bowing their knees worshiped him. And when they had mocked him, they took off the purple from him, and put his own clothes on him, and led him out to crucify him (Mark 15:16-20).

That is the story. He was made the butt of the cruel sport of the soldiers: they put a garment of purple upon Him in mockery, because that was the royal color. Then they plaited a crown of thorns. It would be proper for a king to wear a crown, so they made Him a crown of thorns and jammed it upon His head. After that they began to salute Him, "Hail, King of the Jews!" All of this was in derision and mockery, making sport of their prisoner. When they had worn themselves out with this lampooning, they took off the purple robe from Him, and put His own clothes on Him, and led Him away to be crucified.

To read that record is heartrending. I often think my own spiritual life would be strengthened if I would make it a point every now and again to read one of the accounts of the crucifixion. We would do well to keep in mind this is what the Son of God suffered for us. We should not forget it. When we read this account we should remind ourselves that while all of this was going on, His Father in heaven saw it all.

Remember when Peter had wanted Him to refuse to go up to Jerusalem and later had tried to prevent His arrest? Jesus of Nazareth had said to him: "Thinkest thou that I cannot now pray to my Father, and he shall presently give me more than twelve legions of angels?" (Matt. 26:53). We have in mind that while He suffered all this indignity and cruel, coarse behavior, He was the King of Kings: He was the Lord of all. He did not, on His own account, need to accept one thing they did to Him; He could have spoken the word and been rescued by twelve legions of angels. But this is what He came to do. He came to suffer on my account. This should bring on my part a complete commitment to Him in loving appreciation. The Scriptures tell us we were redeemed not by the blood of the lamb but by the precious blood of the Son of God.

> And they compel one Simon a Cyrenian, who passed by, coming out of the country, the father of Alexander and Rufus, to bear his cross (Mark 15:21).

This is the only place where this man is mentioned; and as one thinks about it, there need never be anything else to make him important. He was the man, coming along at that time, who was forced to carry the cross. Jesus of Nazareth was not able to carry His own cross, evidently having been so weakened by the treatment He had received, He could not carry that heavy cross up the hill. So they compelled a stranger from the outside to bear His cross. "And they bring him unto the place Golgotha, which is, being interpreted, The place of a skull" (Mark 15:22). We call it "Calvary's Cross," though every now and again we see that word "Golgotha" mentioned. This was the name of the particular spot where they put up the cross, and we may well keep in mind this was no unusual, fancy place: it was actually the city dump.

"And they gave him to drink wine mingled with myrrh: but he received it not" (Mark 15:23). Apparently the myrrh would have deadened the pain, perhaps as laudanum does. It would have affected Him as a sort of sedative to deaden the pain; but when He tasted it He refused to drink it. He intended to suffer to the fullest everything that was involved in the death I should have died. "And when they had crucified him, they parted his garments, casting lots upon them, what every man should take. (The soldiers cast lots upon His garments; namely, they decided in a gambling fashion who would get the garments.) And it was the third hour, and they crucified him. And the superscription of his accusation was written over, THE KING OF THE JEWS" (Mark 15:24-26).

When we look at the other Gospels we find that the inscription varied some. But also we read as we look at the other Gospels that the inscription was placed over Him in three languages – Hebrew, Greek and Latin. So it is possible the actual wording would differ in the various inscriptions. They all convey the same general message: "And with him they crucify two thieves; the one on his right hand, and the other on his left" (Mark 15:27). This was the normal, official method of execution. In those days a man who was convicted of theft also would be put to death. "And the scripture was fulfilled, which saith, And he was numbered with the transgressors" (Mark 15:28).

> And they that passed by railed on him, wagging their heads, and saying, Ah, thou that destroyest the temple, and buildest it in three days, save thyself, and come down from the cross. Likewise also the chief priests mocking said among themselves with the scribes, He saved others; himself he cannot save. Let Christ the King of Israel descend now from the cross, that we may see and believe. And they that were crucified with him reviled him (Mark 15:29-32).

During all this ridicule these people did not realize: they did not recognize that He could not save Himself. He died to save me. He could not come down from the cross: He went there to die on my account. It was necessary for Him to go through with it.

> And when the sixth hour was come, there was darkness over the whole land until the ninth hour (Mark 15:33).

There was darkness for three hours.

> And at the ninth hour Jesus cried with a loud voice, saying, Eloi, Eloi, la-ma sa-bach-tha-ni? which is, being interpreted, My God, my God, why hast thou forsaken me? (Mark 15:34).

Many people have wondered about that outcry. This is the quotation from the first verse of Psalm 22. In John 19:30 the last words He spoke on the cross were, "It is finished." Many people feel that when Jesus of Nazareth was dying He was repeating the 22nd Psalm, in which is found the most detailed description of the agonies of death by crucifixion in all Scripture.

Chapter 56

EVENTS FROM THE CROSS TO THE GRAVE

(Mark 15:38-47)

There is much to be learned by noting the people who were present at the crucifixion of Jesus of Nazareth. We may note the cold, subtle hatred of the leaders who wanted Him killed. It may be hard to understand, but there it was. We may note the unstable and confused mind of Pilate who did not know for sure what to do, because he did not want to condemn Him. He finally decided to act in line with the demands of the people in his own self interest. Then there was the callous, brutal conduct of the soldiers as they made sport of Him, finally even casting lots to see who would get His clothes. There was the shaken uncertainty of His disciples as they fled into obscurity. Then, too, there was the sarcastic ridicule of the mob as He was dying. He was also mocked by the chief priests. And there was the repentant thief hanging beside Him who cried out, "Lord, remember me when thou comest into thy kingdom." Then there was the centurion who, when Jesus of Nazareth had cried with a loud voice and had given up the ghost, said: "Truly this man was the Son of God." Also there were the faithful women who stayed with Him to the last, watching from afar.

But we may take special note of something else. Joseph of Arimathea came and boldly asked for the body of Jesus of Nazareth that he might put Him in his own grave. Nicodemus, too, joined Joseph of Arimathea in this last service for the body of Jesus of Nazareth. These are things that come to mind, each of them reminding us of how varied human beings can be – and how incredibly stupid human beings can be, to turn away from the One who loved them and came to give Himself for them.

In addition to these things about the human beings present there were signs in natural events. Matthew tells us there was darkness over the land for three hours from the sixth hour until the ninth hour, which is like saying from noon until three o'clock in the afternoon. This might have been an eclipse. Then there was an earthquake when the graves were opened, and many bodies of the saints which slept arose and came out of the graves after His resurrection and went into the holy city and appeared unto many (Matt. 27:52-53). Many people who read this will not be able to accept it, but there is much having to do with God and with heaven and with the spiritual world that people do not accept. This is the nature of unbelief. In other words, it is surprising how many of us can believe only what we can understand. How limited we are!

> And the veil of the temple was rent in twain from the top to the bottom. And when the centurion, which stood over against him, saw that he so cried out, and gave up the ghost, he said, Truly this man was the Son of God. There were also women looking on afar off: among whom was Mary Magdalene, and Mary the mother of James the less and of Joses, and Salome; (who also, when he was in Galilee, followed him, and ministered unto him;) and many other women which came up with him unto Jerusalem. And now when the even was come, because it was the preparation, that is, the day before the sabbath, Joseph of Arimathea, an honorable counselor, which also waited for the kingdom of God, came, and went in boldly unto Pilate, and craved the body of Jesus (Mark 15:38-43).

Mark does not mention the fact that this man, Joseph of Arimathea, had been a believer but a secret one. He had believed in the Lord and had confidence in Him, but he had not openly confessed it for fear of the Jews. Now this man who had privately really believed and had kept quiet for personal reasons came boldly unto Pilate and asked for the body of Jesus.

> And Pilate marveled if he were already dead: and calling unto him the centurion, he asked him whether he had been any while dead. And when he knew it of the centurion, he gave the body to Joseph. And he bought fine linen, and took him down, and wrapped him in the linen, and laid him in a sepulcher which was hewn out of a rock, and rolled a stone unto the door of the sepulcher (Mark 15:44-46).

This story is profoundly significant. We read elsewhere in the other Gospels several things about this man, Joseph of Arimathea. He was a rich man, he was a counselor whom we would think of as a judge; he was a godly man who trusted in God; but he had kept quiet about his faith. He was not a priest and he was not prominent in religious matters. Boldly he went to Pilate and asked for the body of Jesus Christ. I feel we have in his action a personal response to the situation. It is almost as though he would have said: "When you treat my Lord this way it is impossible for me to be quiet." He came forward openly and identified himself with this broken Man and asked for the body, which Pilate gave to him. Now the body of Jesus of Nazareth was handled by loving and reverent hands. The body was taken down from the cross, wrapped in fine linen.

Chapter 57

THE RESURRECTION

(Mark 16:1-8)

Perhaps the most astonishing feature of the gospel story is the resurrection. Much of what is said about the gospel and emphasized about Christ Jesus, refers to the inner conviction of the heart and soul, the personal acceptance of Jesus Christ in one's own heart and commitment unto Him in one's own soul. No one can really see these actions: we only hear about them. It is easy to fall into the snare of feeling that such is the whole nature of the blessing of God: that it is all inside oneself. But there were aspects of the work of Jesus of Nazareth and aspects of the events that involved Him as told by Mark, that bring these spiritual realities into the open.

> And when the sabbath was past, Mary Magdalene, and Mary the mother of James, and Salome, had bought sweet spices, that they might come and anoint him. And very early in the morning the first day of the week, they came unto the sepulcher at the rising of the sun. And they said among themselves, Who shall roll us away the stone from the door of the sepulcher? And when they looked, they saw that the stone was rolled away: for it was very great. And entering into the sepulcher, they saw a young man sitting on the right side, clothed in a long white garment; and they were affrighted. And he saith unto them, Be not affrighted: Ye seek Jesus of Nazareth, which was crucified: he is risen; he is not here: behold the place where they laid him. But go your way, tell his disciples and Peter that he goeth before you into Galilee: there shall ye see him, as he said unto you. And they went out quickly, and fled from the sepulcher; for they trembled and were amazed: neither said they any thing to any man; for they were afraid (Mark 16:1-8).

As we read this notice exactly how it is reported. There was not a word about the disciples beyond their feeling of fear; no word about what they thought or what their understanding was. The women came to embalm the body in the usual manner. His body had been put in the grave several days before; and during the Sabbath, of course, no one would open the grave. Now the

Sabbath was over and they came to do the usual thing; this would be to anoint the dead body with spices before they wound Him up in His grave clothes, a form of embalming. The women faced a practical problem: they remembered a huge stone had been put in the mouth of the cave. The soldiers had been there to guard it. It had been carefully sealed because word was abroad Jesus was going to rise from the dead. The soldiers had been instructed to be extremely careful that no one disturbed the body, because the rulers did not want anything to happen to the body which would enable people to say He was gone.

When the women came they remembered this fact but it did not stop them from coming. This is a marvelous indication of an attitude that must be acceptable and very pleasing to God. If they had wanted any excuse to keep out of any participation they could simply have said: "We can't do it. The body should be embalmed, but there is a big stone there." Many people, I am sure, would have taken this as an impossible situation. They would not even have started to go to the tomb, and certainly they would not have bought spices to do the work. But when the heart and love are involved, one moves on as if one can do the impossible. They came, knowing not how to surmount this obstacle, the huge stone, but they came. Matthew tells what happened:

> And, behold, there was a great earthquake: for the angel of the Lord descended from heaven, and came and rolled back the stone from the door, and sat upon it (Matt. 28:2).

Mark lets us face the fact that so far as the women were concerned, they expected the stone to be there.

Then comes the astonishing record: the stone had been rolled away. The grave was open. They looked in and saw a young man sitting there in a long white garment. They were "affrighted." (That's an old English way of saying they were literally scared to death.) This was utterly unexpected, actually strange and terrifying. And while they looked the angel said unto them: "Be not affrighted: Ye seek Jesus of Nazareth, which was crucified: (I know why you came, you came about Him) he is risen (oh glorious words); he is not here (of course He is not here): behold the place where they laid him" (Mark 16:6).

Luke tells us that when Peter came and looked into the grave he beheld the linen clothes laid by themselves. That is an interesting point, because it would not be that way if the body had evaporated. Peter took note of the practical fact that those linen clothes were folded and laid away. "But go your way, tell his disciples and Peter that he goeth before you into Galilee: there shall ye see him, as he said unto you" (Mark 16:7).

What a striking message! I try to picture for myself what it would have been like to stand there with a heavy heart in the early morning hour in front of that open grave. I would have come to embalm the body of one whom I had heard, appreciated, believed in and loved. I would have come to share in these last rites, as it were. But now, He was gone! And then this young man gives this message: "Go your way, tell his disciples and Peter that he goeth before you into Galilee: there shall ye see him, as he said unto you." No wonder we read:

> And they went out quickly, and fled from the sepulcher; for they trembled and were amazed: neither said they any thing to any man; for they were afraid (Mark 16:8).

Theirs was a natural reaction. I wonder if we fully appreciate how, in the face of common skepticism, it is such a natural thing to be quiet. There is no use saying anything: no one would believe it anyway.

I wonder if this is what hinders public testimony among believers. Is it true after all, so far as people are concerned, that they believe what they want to hear? And is it also true that people will find it easy to tell what other people want to hear? Would that be one of the things we need to watch? Mark offers no explanation. Other gospel writers offer some of the evidence they were shown that He was really alive, but not Mark. He tells only what happened.

There was a young man in Scotland many years ago, a wealthy young man, who was a student. He was much intrigued with the whole problem of the historicity, the accuracy, of the Bible accounts. This young man knew what was commonly read in the Scriptures and reported in the Bible, and he just wondered if it was true. Since he was skeptical, he organized an expedition and went out to Palestine to dig into the situation there to see if he could not prove that the Gospel of Luke was not true historically. I was an unbeliever then and acquainted with this young student's project. I was tremendously impressed that though William Ramsey had gone to Palestine to prove the Gospel of Luke untrue, he had been convinced that it was. As a result he was converted. He wrote a book on that matter called *Luke*, and in it Sir William Ramsey makes this statement: "The resurrection is the best attested fact in ancient history." We know what that means: in his judgment not one thing we read about ancient times has as much actual support in fact as the resurrection of Jesus Christ from the dead.

Chapter 58

APPEARANCES AFTER THE RESURRECTION

(Mark 16:9-13)

Some aspects of the gospel story are so commonly told we are inclined to take them for granted, even if we do not believe them. Some years ago an interesting cartoon strip was circulated in the newspapers. It had been developed by Robert Ripley and entitled "Believe It Or Not." I remember that in those days our children adopted this slogan whenever they reported anything unbelievable. They would tell some impossible story, and when they saw the unbelief on our faces, they would say, "Well, believe it or not, that's the way it was." This became quite a factor in good social relations amongst us in our home. When we checked on something we had been told, that person would just say, "Believe it or not," inferring they were not going to be responsible for what we thought. You were never held to strict accountability for your veracity, when you said, "Believe it or not," all the pressure was off.

I mention this because I have the feeling that many times in our discussion of the gospel, whether we hear it in Sunday school or from the pulpit, the attitude prevailing would frequently be "Believe it or not; that's the way it is in the Bible." I think about a young man who was preaching in the community where I taught school. I had become a believer and by this time I knew what I believed in the gospel. The young preacher, who was still in seminary, came to this small country charge to preach on Sunday. At that time I was looking forward to going to the mission field. In our conversations I learned that the man did not really believe the Bible. To me it was incredible a man could read the Scriptures and preach these things, when he did not personally believe them.

I will never forget the particular Sunday I have in mind when he preached on Daniel in the lions' den. That man did not even believe there had been a Daniel. I knew, because I had talked to him. He did not even believe there was such a thing as the lions' den; and he certainly did not believe the story. Yet he preached it from the pulpit and it did not seem to make any difference to the people that he did not really believe it. Now if such a man were going to teach the Bible and preach the Bible, what would he say if you took him by his coat lapels, backed him up to a wall, and asked him, "Do you really believe that Daniel was in the lions' den?" The man I have in mind would have said: "Don't get personal. Surely you don't think we have to mean it just because we say it."

I am commenting about this not because of Daniel in the lions' den, nor because that preacher, whose name I do not even remember, did not believe it. I am noting what Mark tells us about the resurrection of the Lord Jesus Christ. And I am wondering, do we really believe it? Is He alive now? When I face this question, and deep down in my heart bring my own consciousness to face this and commit myself, I find I do believe it. If a person does not make up his mind to believe he will not. Believing does not mean that I know and believing does not mean that I have seen. Believing means that I have accepted some report of that which I have not seen but about which I have heard.

> Now when Jesus was risen early the first day of the week, he appeared first to Mary Magdalene, out of whom he had cast seven devils. And she went and told them that had been with him, as they mourned and wept. And they, when they had heard that he was alive, and had been seen of her, believed not (Mark 16:9-11).

Mary Magdalene had been delivered from the powers of evil. This woman had been possessed with seven demons and she knew what it was to be delivered. Her heart was filled with gratitude toward her Savior and she had shared in the sorrow of the crucifixion. She had seen the men put Him in the tomb, and now in deep emotion she had gone there early in the morning but He was not there. When she came away she met Him, and He talked with her. The other Gospels tell us she thought He was the gardener. He gave her a message so she came to them and said, "I have seen Him. He talked with me." These men and women were believers who had also suffered the sorrow and had seen all the things she had seen. Their hearts were heavy, but they did not believe her.

It is no different today. People are still in the company of believers, and they do believe in God. They hear the words of Scripture and think they may be true. They will go along until they come right to this point: is He alive? Someone may testify, "Last night I talked with the Lord"; and I think how easy it is to accept that as a matter of course; in fact, as just a pious comment.

> After that he appeared in another form unto two of them, as they walked, and went into the country. And they went and told it unto the residue: neither believed they them (Mark 16:12-13).

Luke gives the full story and it is quite a story, but it was not really believed. Two disciples were walking toward Emmaus, and a stranger met them and began conversation. They talked with Him and afterward they remembered their hearts did burn within them while He talked and opened to them the Scriptures. They had this experience, and although they had walked several miles to the village where they were to spend the night, after they had their supper, they rushed all the way back into Jerusalem to tell the other disciples they had actually seen the Lord. But the disciples in Jerusalem did not believe them.

As I read this whole passage I wonder why Mark wrote this record. Apparently he did not write it to describe the events. The one thing that Mark seems to underscore is that those disciples in Jerusalem did not believe the story told by the men from Emmaus. Mark is pointing out their natural incredulity. We seldom believe anything in which we have not personally been involved. Apparently this is why Mark recorded it. What they had heard, the disciples did not accept. I emphasize this because I want to warn us about something: when people tell us of personal experiences with God, we should take a sharp hold of our natural feelings because we are just ordinary human beings, and the truth of the matter is we are inclined not to believe them. When we study this we begin to realize this is the condition of natural persons before they have received the Holy Spirit. If our hearts are open to the presence of God, the Holy Spirit will enable us to believe these things. Why should we be careful about this? Because our salvation depends on it. We are saved by believing in Him.

Chapter 59

THE GREAT COMMISSION

(Mark 16:14-18)

Different persons respond in different ways to the gospel. For some the matter of believing, of faith, seems to be a matter of the mind. They want a reason for what they believe, and if it is reasonable they think it is more plausible: that it is easier to believe. For some people believing in the Lord is a matter of the heart, or their emotions. They are lonely and they love His companionship; they are afraid and they love His assurance; and so they put their trust in Him.

For some people the matter of believing in Christ seems to be a matter of experience. Certain things happen to them. Events take place in their lives and because of these events they believe in the Lord Jesus Christ. No one of these approaches excludes the other. Those who believe faith to be a matter of reason can be comforted and can see power working but it is for them primarily a matter of reason. There are no doubt other ways of believing than those I have sketched, but this will bring to our minds the thought that different people have different ways of responding to the call of God in Christ Jesus.

I have commented on the style of Mark and have pointed out that in the course of this text there are practically no arguments. Mark does not try to make his report especially reasonable to anyone. There is no personal feeling: he is not seeking to comfort or to assure. He is simply telling it. His record is mainly a matter of action, or telling events just the way they are. This may help us to understand how he reported the Great Commission which Jesus of Nazareth gave to His disciples. Each of the four Gospels has a version of this command of the Lord. I suspect the one with which we are most familiar is found in Matthew.

> And Jesus came and spake unto them, saying, All power is given unto me in heaven and in earth. Go ye therefore, and teach all nations, baptizing them in the name of the Father, and of the Son, and of the Holy Ghost: teaching them to observe all things whatsoever I have commanded you: and,

> lo, I am with you always, even unto the end of the world. Amen (Matt. 28:18-20).

We feel when we have heard this, we have heard it all. That is what we are told to do. Here are our marching orders.

> And he said unto them, Go ye into all the world, and preach the gospel to every creature. He that believeth and is baptized shall be saved; but he that believeth not shall be damned. And these signs shall follow them that believe; In my name shall they cast out devils; they shall speak with new tongues; they shall take up serpents; and if they drink any deadly thing, it shall not hurt them; they shall lay hands on the sick, and they shall recover (Mark 16:15-18).

This seems different from the report by Matthew but in substance it is the same thing. Now let us note how Luke reports what Jesus of Nazareth told them:

> And said unto them, Thus it is written, and thus it behooved Christ to suffer, and to rise from the dead the third day: and that repentance and remission of sins should be preached in his name among all nations, beginning at Jerusalem. And ye are witnesses of these things. And, behold, I send the promise of my Father upon you: but tarry ye in the city of Jerusalem, until ye be endued with power from on high (Luke 24:46-49).

The same message is reported by John but with still a different emphasis:

> Then said Jesus to them again, Peace be unto you: as my Father hath sent me, even so send I you. And when he had said this, he breathed on them, and saith unto them, Receive ye the Holy Ghost: whosesoever sins ye remit, they are remitted unto them; and whosesoever sins ye retain, they are retained (John 20:21-23).

We may see a still different emphasis when we read further in John:

> So when they had dined, Jesus saith to Simon Peter, Simon, son of Jonas, lovest thou me more than these? He saith unto him, Yea, Lord; thou knowest that I love thee. He saith unto him, Feed my lambs. He saith to him again the second time, Simon, son of Jonas, lovest thou me? He saith unto him, Yea, Lord: thou knowest that I love thee. He saith unto him, Feed my sheep. He saith unto him the third time, Simon, son of Jonas, lovest thou me? Peter was grieved because he said unto him the third time, Lovest thou me? And he said unto him, Lord, thou knowest all things; thou knowest that I love thee. Jesus saith unto him, Feed my sheep (John 21:15-17).

It would be well to make a note of these passages and compare them from time to time. Each has a statement that includes the final instructions from our Lord to His disciples.

> Afterward he appeared unto the eleven as they sat at meat, and upbraided them with their unbelief and hardness of heart, because they believed not them which had seen him after he was risen (Mark 16:14).

The Lord notices how the hearts of the believers respond to the testimony of others. I should learn from this fact. When someone bears witness and testimony to what the Lord has done for him, how does it affect me? When someone tells of some powerful answer to prayer, does it leave me cold? Do I realize the Lord notices these things? He upbraided the unbelieving disciples. The Lord wants us to listen to each other.

> And he said unto them, Go ye into all the world, and preach the gospel to every creature. He that believeth and is baptized shall be saved; but he that believeth not shall be damned (Mark 16:15-16).

That is the Scripture: the preaching of the gospel is significant and those who listen will either be saved or condemned. There is no "no-man's land." Everyone has sinned; the only people who will not be condemned and destroyed are the people who believe in the Lord Jesus Christ. So the preaching is set out, and those who believe will be saved and those who do not believe will be condemned. Preaching the gospel will be effectual, one way or the other.

"And these signs shall follow them that believe" (Mark 16:17-18). Souls do not believe because of these signs: but these signs will follow them that believe. The signs will occur after people believe. Now if I hear the gospel and believe it, and then no signs follow in my life, what am I to think? It is like a person building a fire and there is no smoke; or a person planting a shrub and there are no leaves; what would one think? We know what any person would think, and he would be right. If I hear the gospel and believe it to be true, and nothing happens, it is because what I heard was anemic: a pale version of the gospel.

Why should anyone want to discredit the authenticity of these sentences? There are people who claim they are not in the original text. These signs have all been mentioned one way or another in the Gospels. I wonder if such attempt is a lame effort to excuse their own weak testimony. This is a sobering line of thought. The truth is plain: the preaching of the gospel is by the authority of God, and if it is done as God wants it done there will be signs following.

Chapter 60

THE ASCENSION

(Mark 16:19-20)

> So then after the Lord had spoken unto them, he was received up into heaven, and sat on the right hand of God. And they went forth, and preached every where, the Lord working with them, and confirming the word with signs following. Amen (Mark 16:19-20).

What a simple, eloquent finale to the career of Jesus of Nazareth upon earth! In this short, compact narrative of the Gospel of Mark, in these sixteen chapters he has set forth a simple record of what happened. After Jesus of Nazareth had spoken unto His disciples: we know this is what He came to do, we know this is what He did. He would not talk forever, on and on into eternity: He was finished. There is a message. The message has limits, and those limits are to be felt even in preaching.

> I must work the works of him that sent me, while it is day: the night cometh, when no man can work (John 9:4).

Work while we have the light, we will not have it all the time. I fear this urgency is often missed in our preaching, and in our teaching and often in our Bible study. We accent and emphasize the everlasting grace and kindness of God, but we are in danger of letting people get the idea they can ignore the Lord, insult Him by their indifference, turn away, and things will still be all right. We leave the impression everything will be fine; He is going to take care of them anyway. Thus people get a mistaken view of what grace means. They seem to imply that because God is gracious He will not check up on anyone.

But notice what is going on in the world. Things in the world come to an end. Why should anyone think that God, who made this world, who created it, and put natural limits to everything that moves, will go on and on in dealing with people, and never come to a point of pulling the string on them? At the time of the flood the Scripture records the Word of God, "My spirit shall not always strive with man." This is still true. I do not have forever to hear the call of God if I pay no attention. We are given to understand that when He had done what He came to do, when He had said what He came to say, He was finished. And He sat down at the right hand of God, waiting for the next phase to take place.

This is more fully described in Acts 1:1-12. He sat down at the right hand of God and He is there now with honor and with authority. We know that from there beside the Father, He sent forth His Holy Spirit into the hearts of believers, when the Day of Pentecost occurred. From there He will come again in the clouds of heaven and in great glory as the Scriptures teach.

> And they went forth, and preached every where, the Lord working with them, and confirming the word with signs following. Amen (Mark 16:20).

When anyone today asks why we have foreign missions we can tell him because the Lord said, "Go." All over the world men and women are going. In every country, wherever there is a group of believing people, someone is going out as a missionary to the ends of the earth with this gospel story. That is what they have been told to do.

Let us not misunderstand this. Let us not think the way we do the will of God is by going out to see how much good we can do; by giving water to the thirsty, food to the hungry and a place to sleep to them who are cold. All of that is good and helpful in the way of indicating the nature of the love of God; but that is not what we were told to do. There is nothing against such charitable work but that isn't all: we were told to preach, to tell. We were to tell the whole wide world what God has done, and what He will do in and through Jesus Christ for the salvation of each individual person who will put his or her trust in Him. We are to tell people to put their trust in Him and they will be called into fellowship with Him and with one another.

In Matthew we read: "I will be with you always, even unto the end of the world." Ministers and teachers who are going today often find situations so discouraging, they would have no inward spirit to move on if it were not that they are moved inwardly by the Holy Spirit of God who is quietly and assuredly telling them nothing is too hard for the Lord.

He promised to make the Word increase. "My word shall not return unto me void" (Isa. 55:11). When a man preaches and teaches the truth about Jesus Christ, the Son of God, this Word is like seed. It gets into the heart, and by the grace of God it grows and grows until it is strong in faith, turning that whole soul to God. When He gave them the Word and it increased,

He also gave them certain manifestations of power to confirm their witness as true, as He had promised. The Lord working with them confirmed the Word with signs following. These signs may or may not all take place with every believer as they do with everyone else. You may or may not see any or all of them, but whether you see them or not does not change the fact: these signs are to take place.

These signs are not the whole truth: they are only *signs* of the truth. They are just symbols of the truth. They picture something. But the *truth* is what goes on and what will be confirmed. When we talk about this I could raise a question I think is proper: wherever you go to church, as you hear the gospel preached and hear the gospel talked about in that Sunday school class, are there signs following? Is there evidence of the power of God? Are changes being brought about in the lives of the people? This would confirm the Word. And so, we have been following this record of the life and the work, the death and the resurrection of Jesus Christ, the Son of God, to the glory of His Name.